The Smart Parent Gu

Scholarships, Grants,

Smart Parent Independent Publishers

Table of Contents

INTRODUCTION

This publication details financial aid options for high school students who plan to attend college, undergraduates who have chosen a major, undergraduate and graduate students who would like to pursue a graduate or professional degree program. Obtaining a college education is a lengthy and expensive endeavor. The cost of your education should be evaluated over the total length of time it will take to obtain your degree. Students, who plan on pursuing graduate or professional degrees, should include those costs in their estimates.

There are many financial aid programs that help to students to attend college. Private and federal financial aid sources are available for almost every field of study.

More than 6,500 colleges participate in the U.S. Department of Educations' student financial aid programs. The U.S. Department of Education provided more than $105 billion in financial support to students last year.

Private individuals, alumni, corporations and religious organizations donated more than $27 billion to America's Colleges and Universities.

THE VALUE OF A COLLEGE DEGREE

The value of a college degree has been contested, analyzed and studied with a cynical viewpoint as the cost of a college education has continued to rise. College tuition and fees rose more than 400 percent in the last 25 years. In fact, it cost more than $51,000 to attend George Washington University in Washington DC in 2009.

Despite the rising cost, investing in a college education pays major dividends. High school graduates can expect to earn about $1.5 million over the course of their work life. College graduates with a bachelor's degree will earn around $2.7 million.

Students who earned a master's degree made an average of $71,236 in 2008. Master's degree holders earn about $3.2 million over the course of their life. College graduates with doctoral degrees (PhD) earned an average of $99,995 in 2008. Doctoral degree (PhD) holders earn nearly $4.5 million over the course of their work life.

Students who go on to earn a professional degree, like a Law (JD) or Medical degree (MD) will see their earnings rise as well. The U.S Census bureau reported that the average earnings of graduates with professional degrees were $125,622. Professional degrees holders earn about $5.6 million over the course of their work life.

FIRST YEAR SALARIES

Despite the down economy, there are still many professions where the demand for new college graduates, in specific industries, continues to grow.

While America has a 10% unemployment rate, college graduates have an unemployment rate of just 4%. In fact, over the past decade, personnel income has declined in America. Median income in the United States was just $49,777 in 2009.

The competitive nature of the global economy promotes rapid computerization of the most mundane industries. Without notice we are confronted with computers even as we do something as simple as shopping for groceries.

In January of 2011, Google announced that they planned to add more than 6,200 new employees this year. Google spent more than $2 Billion in December 2010 by providing every employee with a $1,000 tax free Christmas bonus in addition to a 10 percent salary increase.

Today, in many instances, starting salary offers for new college graduates exceed the median earnings of $49,777 for most American workers. There are a number of industries where the demand for knowledgeable candidates is growing at rapid pace.

Accounting

The demand for accountants and auditors is expected to grow by 22 percent. More than 279,400 new accounting positions are projected by 2018. Business expansion, greater government regulation will drive job growth. First year salary offers to new accounting graduates were $47,982 in 2010.

Finance

The complexity and global diversification of investments, hedge fund growth and the rapid expansion of new markets, will spur the need for more financial analysts to research and recommend profitable strategies. The demand for financial analysts is expected to grow 20 percent. First year salary offers to finance grads were $49,607 in 2010.

Engineering

Overall employment for engineers is expected to grow by 178,300 new jobs over the decade. The employment of engineers in engineering, research and development, and consulting should account for most of the demand. First year salary offers to new engineering graduates were $55,067 in 2010.

Computer Science,Video Game Development

The University of California San Diego estimates that 200 million people play video games online monthly. The demand for computer software engineers is expected to increase 32 percent by 2018. More than 295,000 new positions are expected to be created over the next decade. New internet technologies help to increase demand for computer software engineers who can develop Internet applications and software. The demand for knowledgeable computer software engineers is further enhanced as electronic data-processing systems in business, telecommunications, healthcare, government become more complex. Computer multi-media artists and animators averaged $56,330 in salary in 2010. First year salary offers to computer science degree graduates were $61,205 in 2010.

Health Care

Employment in the healthcare industry is projected to increase 22 percent. The rapid growth of the elderly population accounts for most of the new demand. The healthcare industry will generate 3.2 million jobs by 2018. Medical and Health Services Managers averaged $80,240 in salary in 2010. First year salary offers to Registered Nurses averaged $62,450.

Database Mining & Database Engineering

The employment of computer network, systems, and database administrators is projected to grow by 286,600 new jobs, or 30 percent over the next decade. Database Administrators averaged $69,740 in salary in 2010. Network Systems and Data Communication Analysts averaged $71,100 last year.

HOW TO USE THIS GUIDE

Read the listings to determine which organizations offer financial assistance to students like you. If there is any doubt as to whether you are a qualified applicant or if that organization provides financial assistance to students in your major, write them for a definitive answer. If for some reason you do not qualify for assistance, strive to earn the scholarship, grant or fellowship the following year. Most organizations provide financial assistance to students in many different categories. Apply to any and all organizations that may be able to help you. Most groups provide grants until funds are depleted.

Remember, you are only competing with students who have this information and who have applied.

Start researching scholarship programs with the assistance of your parent today. (Some organizations identify students in the 8th grade.)

Read and carefully examine the program requirements for students. In many cases students do not to apply to programs that they are eligible for due to misinterpretation of program guidelines.

Use a checklist to assemble the documents requested by the sponsoring organization. Most organizations don't have the time or the resources to respond or return incomplete applications. Proofread all documents carefully before you seal the envelope.

PHILANTHROPY AND EDUCATION

W.E.B Dubois
B.A. Fisk University, B.A., M.A., PhD Harvard

Financial assistance in the form of scholarships, grants, and fellowships for African American students has been available for many years. Often these funds were allocated in response to charges of discrimination made against particular universities and other establishment institutions. After the Civil War, a number of foundations were established to help rebuild the South. In many instances these funds prohibited contributions to Negroes. The Peabody Education Fund at Vanderbilt University is an example.

The Slater Fund was established in 1882 for the education of Freedmen. John Fox Slater donated $1,000,000 in 1882 to establish the John F. Slater Fund for the Education of Freedmen. The Slater Fund was instrumental in supporting, Spelman Seminary, Fisk University, Hampton University, Tuskegee Institute, Fisk University, Claflin University, and the Slater State Normal and Industrial School (Winston-Salem State University).

The chairman of the Slater Fund was former President Rutherford Hayes. President Hayes thought the chance of locating worthy candidates for financial support was nonexistent. Despite his belief that blacks were not suited for advanced study, Hayes was quoted to say, "If there is any young colored man in the South whom we find to have a talent for art or literature or any special aptitude for study, we are willing to give him money from the education fund to send him to Europe to give him advanced education." ´Boston Herald, November 2, 1890.

Dubois wrote to Hayes to request a scholarship since he met those qualifications. His request went unanswered. Dubois accused the President of defaming African Americans since the fund had no intention of providing scholarships for Negroes. The fund and its board were being used as a pulpit from which to make the claim that Negroes were only suited for industrial education. Dubois challenged the integrity of the board since they had not awarded funds to any students. Dubois received the Master of Arts degree from Harvard University in 1892 and continued to forward letters of recommendation to Rutherford Hayes. Through his persistence and scholarship, the Slater fund awarded Dubois $750 to finance a year of study in Europe at the University of Heidelberg. W.E.B. Dubois went on to earn his PhD. in Sociology from Harvard University.

Philanthropist, Matal Lawson Jr.

There are many well known individuals and organizations that assist students attend and complete their college education by providing scholarships, grants and fellowships.

The majority of scholarship contributions come from everyday individuals who contribute due to their faith, personal ethic, or desire to see others succeed where they were denied an opportunity. Mr. Matal Lawson of the Ford Motor Company donated more than $1.2 million over his lifetime to provide scholarships for students. Mr. Matal Lawson was a Ford Motor Company fork lift driver for more than 50 years. An African American, Matal Lawson Jr. was born in Shreveport, Louisiana in 1921 during a time in America where oppression and racial discrimination were the norm. As a child born during the Great Depression, Mr. Lawson was only able to complete the 9th grade. Mr. Lawson made his first major contribution in 1991 after watching the Michigan UNCF telethon.

He contributed $30,000 to the UNCF at that time. Over the next five years he contributed more than $200,000 to the charity. Mr. Lawson later established endowed scholarships at Wayne State University and Louisiana State University at Shreveport.

Jack Kent Cooke Foundation
44325 Woodridge Parkway
Lansdowne, Virginia 20176
www.jkcf.org

Jack Kent Cooke was born during the Great Depression, and unable to afford the cost to attend college. Jack Kent Cooke began his career as a door to door encyclopedia salesman to help support his family. His best customers were all college graduates or business owners who hoped to prepare their children for college. His experiences as a salesman left a lifelong impression on Jack Kent Cooke. By his bequest the Jack Kent Cooke Foundation was established with the sale of the Washington Redskins and the rest of his billion dollar estate.

In 2009, the Jack Kent Cooke Foundation provided financial support and assistance to more than 700 students.

The Young Scholars Program of the JKCF identifies outstanding students in the 7th and 8th grades with financial need. Financial assistance, mentoring, and academic support services are provided for outstanding students. Scholarships are awarded through completion of the Bachelor's degree. Young Scholar Program students are eligible to apply for Graduate Scholarships as well.

The Jack Kent Cooke Foundation's Undergraduate Transfer Scholarship provides up to $30,000 per year to 50 outstanding two-year and community college students. Undergraduate Transfer Scholars are also eligible to apply for Graduate Scholarships of up to $50,000

Flip Wilson

Flip Wilson was born Clerow Wilson Jr. in 1933. Flip Wilson was one of eighteen children. Flip spent many years in reform school and foster homes before he joined the U.S. Air Force in 1949. A natural entertainer, Flip was soon touring military bases to uplift his fellow servicemen. He left the military in 1954 and by 1960 he was a regular at the Apollo, the Tonight Show, Laugh In and the Ed Sullivan Show. The Flip Wilson Show first aired in 1970.

Flip Wilson went on to win Golden Globe, Emmy and Grammy Awards as an entertainer.

The Flip Wilson Memorial Journalism Scholarships were established with the support of his publicist Kathleen Fearn-Banks. Ms Kathleen Fearn-Banks is on the faculty of the University of Washington. Ms Fearn-Banks is a member of the Delta Sigma Theta Sorority Inc.

The Flip Wilson Memorial Journalism Scholarships offers $21,449 to cover one year of tuition, room and board books and fees. Students in their senior year who attend Rutgers University, the University of Washington, Wayne State University, and Howard University in Washington, D.C. are eligible to apply.

UNITED NEGRO COLLEGE FUND

The United Negro College Fund (UNCF) was incorporated on April 25, 1944 by Mary McLeod Bethune, founder and president of Bethune Cookman College and Frederick D. Patterson, who was president of Tuskegee Institute. The United Negro College Fund (UNCF) provides college tuition money and scholarships for 39 private historically black colleges and universities.

Many of the students (60%), that the United Negro College Fund supports, are the first in their families to attend college. The majority of the scholarships recipients of the United Negro College Fund have exceptional financial need; most (62%) have annual family incomes of less than $25,000. The United Negro College Fund (UNCF) awarded $113 million in grants and scholarships to more than 65,000 students in 2005.

UNCF Colleges & Universities

Allen University
Benedict College
Bennett College
Bethune-Cookman
Claflin University
Clark Atlanta
Dillard University
Edward Waters
Fisk University
Florida Memorial
Huston-Tillotson
Jarvis Christian College,
Johnson C. Smith
Lane College
LeMoyne-Owen College
Livingstone College
Miles College
Morehouse College
Morris College
Oakwood University
Paine College
Paul Quinn College
Philander Smith
Rust College
Saint Augustine's
Saint Paul's College
Shaw University
Spelman College
Stillman College
Talladega College
Texas College
Tougaloo College
Tuskegee University
Virginia Union University
Voorhees College
Wilberforce University
Wiley College
Xavier University

Gates Millennium Scholars Program
The United Negro Scholarship Fund
8260 Willow Oaks Corporate Drive
P.O. Box 10444, Fairfax, VA 22031
www.gmsp.org
1-877-690-4677

The Gates Millennium Scholars initiative, funded by a grant from the Bill & Melinda Gates Foundation and administered by the United Negro College Fund and partners is aimed at expanding access and opportunity to higher education to those citizens who will help reflect the diverse society in which we live. The Gates Millennium Scholars awards will enable 20,000 young Americans to attend undergraduate and graduate institutions of their choice and be prepared to assume important roles as leaders in their professions and in their communities. Bill and Melinda Gates Foundation have established this initiative to encourage and support students in completing college and in continuing on to earn the master's and doctorate degrees in disciplines where ethnic and racial groups are currently underrepresented. The scholarships will be renewed yearly if recipients maintain a 3.0 grade average. Financial assistance is available for graduate students in mathematics, science (including life sciences, physical sciences and computer science), engineering, and education. Scholarship awards include full tuition, room, board, books and materials.

Isaiah West, Future Surgeon

Isaiah West, a June 2010 graduate of Frank W. Ballou High School in Washington DC has been offered more than $1 million to attend college.

The former running back decided not to try out for the football team to devote more time to study. Isaiah plans to be a surgeon. His study paid off.

Isaiah was awarded $200,000 to attend George Washington University. He had similar offers from Duke University and Emory University in Atlanta. Isaiah also received offers from Tulane, Temple and Johns Hopkins University. Isaiah West was also one of 1,000 students nationwide to win the Gates Millennium Scholarship.

Alyssia Clore

Alyssia Clore graduated from the South Atlanta School of Health, Medicine & Sciences in June, 2010. She was one of 1,000 students to win a Gate Millennium Scholarship.

As a Gates Scholar, Alyssia Clore will receive a full tuition scholarship, room and board fees and mentoring for as long as she attends school. Ms. Clore's scholarship is worth more than $500,000 at current tuition rates. Alyssia Clore will attend Spelman College in Atlanta this fall. Alyssia plans to major in biology and then pursue a Ph.D.

Maya Mundell, $1.15 million in Scholarships

Maya Mundell, a graduate in the 2010 class of Northeast High School in Pasadena, Maryland was awarded more than $1.15 million in scholarships to attend college. Maya was offered full scholarships to attend Cornell University, Albright College and The New School. Maya was accepted at Spelman College, Johns Hopkins and American University. Maya plans to attend Cornell University in the fall.

Ms Mundell, who graduated with a 4.1 GPA, was also awarded the prestigious Gates Millennium Scholarship.

Leuk Woldeyohannes, Wheaton High (MD)

In June 2010, Wheaton Maryland High School student, Leuk Woldeyohannes was awarded a Gates Millennium Scholarship. Leuk's mother, a physician, died of cancer when he was 9 years of age. Leuk plans to become physician as well. After earning an "A" in AP Biology, Leuk applied for the Gates scholarship. A member of Wheaton's bioscience academy, Leak was also an intern at the Howard Hughes Medical Institute. The Gates Scholarship covers all undergraduate college expenses. Leuk Woldeyohannes plans to attend Cornell University.

FEDERAL FINANCIAL AID PROGRAMS

Pell Grants

Pell Grants are need based financial awards for Bachelors degree students. Students must be enrolled at least part-time. Pell Grant amounts are based on the financial ability of parents to meet the educational requirements of their student. The maximum Pell Grant award for the 2010 award year is $5,550. Pell grants do not prohibit awardees from receiving other financial aid. Federal Pell Grants do not have to be repaid.

Supplemental Educational Opportunity Grant

The Federal Supplemental Educational Opportunity Grant (FSEOG) program is for undergraduates with exceptional financial need. Students and families with the greatest financial need are eligible for these awards. Students should file for these awards as soon as possible as universities and colleges have limited funding. Grants of $100 to $4,000 are provided to students who qualify for the (FSEOG) program.

College Work Study

College Word Study provides paid employment to assist students in meeting educational expenses. Undergraduate and Graduate students are eligible to participate. The amount of the work award is based on the financial need of the student and the availability of funds. Work hours and compensation vary by institution. Compensation must be at or exceed the federal minimum wage. The amount of compensation you receive is limited by the parameters of the work award. Students are encouraged to apply early.

Perkins Loans

Perkins Loans can be used for undergraduate or graduate study and must be repaid upon matriculation. Undergraduate students may borrow up to $5,500 per year for to finance 4 years of college or university study. Graduate students may borrow up to $8,000 per year for graduate or professional study. The total loan amount can't exceed $60,000. Repayment must begin nine months after graduation.

Stafford Loans

Direct Stafford Loans are low-interest loans for eligible students to help cover the cost of higher education at a four-year college or university, community college, or trade, career, or technical school. Eligible students borrow directly from the U.S. Department of Education. Direct Subsidized Loans are for students with financial need. Eligible students must complete the Free Application for Federal Student Aid. The school will determine the amount you can borrow. Students can borrow up to $57,500. Interest does not accrue during grace periods, or as long as the student is enrolled at least part time.

National SMART Grant

The National Science and Mathematics Access to Retain Talent Grant are available to eligible students during the junior and senior years of undergraduate study. The grant is available to students who major in critical foreign languages, mathematics, engineering, physics, computer science, information systems, chemistry, life and physical sciences. A 3.0 minimum grade point average is necessary for consideration. The National SMART Grant awards $4,000. Students must maintain their academic performance to renew the grant for the second year.

TEACH Grant Program

The TEACH Grant is available to eligible students who agree teach in low income areas. The grant is available to who agree to teach in a public or private elementary or secondary school that serves students from low-income families. Students who major in Mathematics, Science, Bilingual Education and English Language Acquisition and Special Education are eligible to participate in the TEACH Grant Program

Undergraduate and graduate students are eligible. A 3.0 minimum grade point average is necessary for consideration. The TEACH Grant program awards $4,000 to deserving students. Students must maintain their academic performance to renew the grant for the second year.

HIGH SCHOOL STUDENT SCHOLARSHIPS

Intel Science Talent Search Scholarship
1719 N Street, NW
Washington, DC 20036
www.societyforscience.org
www.sciserv.org

The Science Talent Search has been recognizing outstanding students and their research submissions and science projects since 1942.

Today, Intel is the sponsor of the national scientific competition. The Science Talent Search is the most prestigious pre-college science contest in America.

High school seniors in the United States and American students attending school abroad are eligible to participate. Each year, approximately 2000 students complete an entry for the Intel Science Talent Search. The Intel Science Talent Search winner is awarded a $100,000 scholarship.

Intel contributes more than $1.25 million each year for the scholarship program. Many Universities and College provide additional academic incentives to Intel Science Talent Search semi-finalists and finalist.

Jackie Robinson Foundation
One Hudson Square
75 Varick Street, 2nd Floor
New York, NY 10013-1917
www.jackierobinson.org
(212) 290-8600

The Jackie Robinson Foundation provides financial assistance to minority high school students who wish to acquire a college education. The centerpiece of the Jackie Robinson Foundation is its unique Education and Leadership Development Program. The Foundation provides ongoing academic support and mentoring services to students in order insure that Jackie Robinson Scholars reach their full potential as leaders and students. The Jackie Robinson Foundation has provided $43 million in support and scholarship grants for deserving students. The Jackie Robinson Foundation awards students scholarships of up to $7,500 to attend the four year college or university of their choice. The scholarships are renewable for up to 4 years.
There are more than 1,000 Jackie Robinson Foundation scholar alumni.

NAACP Education Department
4805 Mt. Hope Drive
Baltimore, MD 21215-3297
www.naacp.org

The Roy Wilkins Scholarships provides financial assistance to minority students in their senior year of high school or in their first two years of college or university. Scholarships of $2000-$3000 are awarded.

National Honor Society Scholarship Program
National Honor Society
1904 Association Drive
Reston, Virginia 22091
www.nhs.us

The National Honor Society recognizes and rewards outstanding student achievement. The National Honor Society has awarded more than $10 million in scholarships over the years. More than $200,000 in scholarships is awarded annually. The National Honor Society Scholarship Program provides financial assistance to high school seniors who are members of the National Honor Society.

Coca-Cola Scholars Foundation, Inc
P.O. Box 442
Atlanta, GA 30301-0442
www.coca-cola.com/scholars

The Coca-Cola Scholars Foundation provides financial assistance to high school seniors planning to attend college. Coca-Cola Scholars are eligible for awards based on leadership, character, academic record and extracurricular activities. Awards will partially reflect the demographic profiles of selection districts. Semifinalists submit a second application, including an essay, secondary school report and recommendations. Fifty $20,000 scholarships and 100 $4,000 scholarships are awarded for four years.

United States Senate Youth Program
William Randolph Hearst Foundation
90 New Montgomery Street, Suite 1212
San Francisco, CA 94015-4504
Phone: (415) 543-4057 or (800) 841-7048

William Randolph Hearst Foundation
300 West 57th Street, 26th Floor
New York, New York 10019-3741
Telephone: 212-586-5404
www.hearstfdn.org

The United States Senate Youth Program was established in 1962 by U.S. Senate Resolution. The United States Senate Youth Program provides financial assistance to high school juniors and seniors who hold elective office in student government. Student leaders from every state, the District of Columbia spend a week in Washington seeing their national government in action. The Students visit and observe Capitol Hill, the White House, Supreme Court, Pentagon and State Department. Upon completion of the program, each student will be awarded a $5,000 undergraduate scholarship.

Greater Washington Urban League Scholarships
3501 14th Street, NW
Washington, DC 20010
www.gwulparentcenter.org
(202) 265-8200

The Safeway/Greater Washington Urban League Scholarship is awarded to graduating high schools students who reside in the service area of the Washington Urban League. To be eligible for the scholarship, applicants must complete an essay on a subject selected by the sponsors. Applicants must have a minimum 3.20 Grade Point Average and have completed 90% of their school district's community service requirement. The scholarship awards $3,000.

American Dream Scholarship Program
The Sallie Mae Fund
www.thesalliemaefund.org

The Sallie Mae Fund American Dream Scholarship offers $500 to $5,000 to African-American students. The scholarship is open to incoming freshmen as well as undergraduate students. The Sallie Mae Fund has awarded more than $15.5 million in scholarships to more than 6,350 students.

Hallie Q. Brown Scholarship Fund
National Association of Colored Women's Clubs
5808 16th Street, NW. Washington, DC 20011
nacwc.org

The National Association of Colored Women's Clubs provides financial assistance to minority students who have completed at least one semester of postsecondary education, with a minimum GPA of 2.0. Grants are awarded to worthy students.

National Merit Scholarship Corporation
National Achievement Scholarship Program
1560 Sherman Avenue, Suite 200
Evanston, IL 30201
(847) 860-5100
www.nationalmerit.org

The National Achievement Scholarship Program seeks to identify and recognize outstanding black secondary students and provide financial assistance to award winners. The NMSC supports students who have taken the PSAT and the SAT at the designated times. The National Merit Scholarship Corporation provides over 775 scholarships, in varying amounts to African American students.

Taylor Michael's Scholarship Fund
Magic Johnson Foundation, Inc.
6167 Bristol Parkway, Suite 450
Culver City, CA 90230
www.magicjohnson.org

The Taylor Michael's Scholarship Fund provides support for deserving inner-city high school students who demonstrate high academic achievement. The Taylor Michael's Scholarship Fund seeks to make awards to students who may not have been able to afford a college education. Students who are residents of Atlanta, Cleveland, Houston, Los Angeles, and New York are eligible to apply. Scholarship recipients will be selected on the basis of a written essay, and cumulative grade point average.

Congressional Black Caucus Foundation
1720 Massachusetts Ave., NW DC 20036
www.cbcfinc.org

The Congressional Black Caucus Spouses Education Fund provides financial assistance to deserving students of high academic achievement. Graduating high school seniors are eligible to apply. Financial assistance is also available for graduate and doctoral students. Student must reside or attend school in a congressional district represented by a member of the Congressional Black Caucus.

Herbert Lehman Scholarships
www.naacpldf.org
99 Hudson Street, Suite 1600
New York, NY 10013

The Herbert Lehman Education Fund provides financial assistance to African Americans entering a college or university with an enrollment of African Americans that is less than 8% of the total undergraduate enrollment. Preference is given to students planning to attend a southern school that was at one time segregated.

ART SCHOLARSHIPS

Doris & John Carpenter Scholarship
The United Negro Scholarship Fund
8260 Willow Oaks Corporate Drive
P.O. Box 10444, Fairfax, VA 22031
www.uncf.org

The Doris & John Carpenter Scholarship, funded by a $2.9 million endowment, provide renewable scholarships to UNCF students with the greatest demonstrated financial need.

U.S. Department of Education
Jacob K. Javits Fellowship Program
400 Maryland Avenue, SW
Washington, DC 20202-5251
www2.ed.gov/programs/jacobjavits/index.html

The Jacob K. Javits Fellowship Program provides fellowships to students of superior academic ability. Jacob K. Javits Fellows are selected on the basis of demonstrated achievement, financial need, and exceptional promise. Students pursuing the Master of Fine Arts are eligible to apply. Jacob K. Javits Fellowships are awarded annually for up to 48 months or the completion of the degree. A stipend of up to $30,000 is awarded. Students pursuing the Master of Fine Arts (MFA) are eligible to apply

Rhythm Nation/Janet Jackson Scholarship
The United Negro Scholarship Fund
8260 Willow Oaks Corporate Drive
P.O. Box 10444, Fairfax, VA 22031
www.uncf.org

The Grammy Award winning artist Janet Jackson created this $395,000 endowed scholarship. Awards are made annually to students majoring in communications, music, performing arts, and the fine arts. Students must be enrolled in a UNCF college or university must demonstrate need, with a minimum 2.5 Grade Point Average. Inquiries must be made to the financial aid office at each school. Scholarship amounts vary. Scholarships of $2,000 are awarded to eligible students.

John Lennon Scholarship Fund
The United Negro Scholarship Fund
8260 Willow Oaks Corporate Drive
P.O. Box 10444, Fairfax, VA 22031
www.uncf.org

Yoko Ono created the John Lennon Scholarship Fund in memory of John Lennon. The income from this $800,000 endowment provides scholarships for UNCF students in the performing arts and communications. Scholarships of up to $5,000 are awarded to eligible students.

Michael Jackson Endowed Scholarship Fund
The United Negro Scholarship Fund
8260 Willow Oaks Corporate Drive
P.O. Box 10444, Fairfax, VA 22031
www.uncf.org

Michael Jackson Scholarship for performing arts, funded by a $1.5 million endowment, provides renewable scholarships to UNCF students majoring in the performing arts, music, dance and communications. Students enrolled in a UNCF college or university, with demonstrated financial need, and a minimum 2.5 Grade Point Average are eligible to apply. Inquiries must be made to the financial aid office at each school. Scholarships of $4,000 are awarded to eligible students.

National Foundation for Advancement of the Arts
NFAA Arts Recognition and Talent Search
800 Brickell Ave., Suite 500
Miami, FL 33131
www.youngarts.org

The National Foundation for Advancement in the Arts (NFAA) was founded in 1981 as a nonprofit arts organization. The Arts Recognition and Talent Search provides financial assistance to high school seniors involved in dance, music, theater, visual arts, film, video, voice photography, jazz and creative writing. The Arts Recognition and Talent Search awards three million dollars in scholarships and $900,000 in cash prizes. The provides financial assistance to high school seniors who would like to pursue a career in the area of dance, music, the visual arts, theater, writing, or film. To be eligible, students must be U.S. citizens between 17 and 18 years old. Scholarships of $3,000 are awarded. Substantial cash prizes are also awarded

The Malcolm X Scholarship Program
The United Negro Scholarship Fund
8260 Willow Oaks Corporate Drive
P.O. Box 10444, Fairfax, VA 22031
www.uncf.org

The Malcolm X Scholarship Program, through a $350,000 endowment fund established by filmmaker Spike Lee with the support from Nike, Benetton Service Corporation Film works, Allen Kilik, and Abkco Music & Records, provides a renewable scholarship to UNCF students. This scholarship is awarded for demonstrated academic excellence, campus and community leadership, and exceptional courage. Scholarships of $4,000 are awarded to eligible students.

ACCOUNTING SCHOLARSHIPS

There approximately 1.3 million accountants working in the United States. Accountants compile, verify, and analyze financial documents necessary for proper fiscal control and informed decision making for academic, government, and corporate and individual clients. Accountants usually complete the Bachelor of Business Administration degree in accounting before beginning their careers. Over the next decade job growth for accountants and auditors is expected to increase by 22 percent.

Using starting salary information compiled by the National Association of Colleges and Employers, bachelor's degree candidates in accounting received starting offers averaging $48,993 a year in July 2009.

In May of 2008 Median annual wages of wage and salary accountants and auditors were $59,430 in May 2008. The middle half of the occupation earned between $45,900 and $78,210. The bottom 10 percent earned less than $36,720, and the top 10 percent earned more than $102,380. Partners in large accounting firms can earn salaries that can exceed $200,000. The median annual wages in industries employing the large numbers of accountants and auditors continue to grow.

American Institute of Certified Public Accountants
1211 Avenue of the Americas
New York, NY 10036
www.aicpa.org

This program provides awards to outstanding minority students to encourage their selection of accounting as a major and their ultimate entry into the profession. Funding is provided by the AICPA Foundation, the New Jersey Society of CPAs and Robert Half International. The American Institute of Certified Public Accountants has provided over $14 million in scholarships to approximately 8,000 accounting scholars. Each year the American Institute of Certified Public Accountants awards more than $400,000 in scholarships to deserving students. Eligible students are awarded scholarships of $2,000 to $12,000. In many cases the grants are renewable.

Quaker Oats Scholarship Program
The United Negro Scholarship Fund
8260 Willow Oaks Corporate Drive
P.O. Box 10444, Fairfax, VA 22031
www.uncf.org

The Quaker Oats Scholarship Program, funded by a $280,000 grant, provides financial assistance to UNCF students pursuing degrees in business administration, accounting, engineering and liberal arts.

CBS Career Horizons Internship/Scholarship
The United Negro Scholarship Fund
8260 Willow Oaks Corporate Drive
P.O. Box 10444, Fairfax, VA 22031
www.uncf.org

This program is funded by a $250,000 grant from CBS Incorporated. It is open to sophomores and juniors enrolled at an historically black college or university with a minimum GPA of 3.0, majoring in accounting, business, finance, marketing, mass communications or journalism. Students participate in a summer internship, receive a $5,000 stipend and an $8,000 scholarship.

Minorities in Government Finance Scholarship
180 North Michigan Avenue, Suite 800
Chicago, IL 60601-7476
www.gfoa.org

The Government Finance Officers Association provides financial assistance to full or part-time upper-division undergraduate or graduate students. Applicants must be students of public administration, governmental accounting finance, political science, economics or business administration, and plan to pursue a career in state or local government finances. Scholarships of $5,000 are awarded.

The Ron Brown Scholars Program
1160 Pepsi Place, Suite 206
Charlottesville, VA 22901
www.ronbrown.org

The Ron Brown Scholar Program awards scholarships to African-American high school seniors who have demonstrated financial need, social commitment, and leadership potential. The scholarship awards $10, 000 annually for four years. The recipients may use the renewable merit-based scholarships to attend the college or University of their choice. Scholars may request that all or a portion of the award be utilized each year of undergraduate study or deferred for graduate study.

National Society of Accountants
NSA Scholarship Foundation
1010 North Fairfax Street
Alexandria, VA 23314
www.nsaact.org
(703) 549-6400

The Scholarship foundation provides financial assistance to Students majoring in accounting with a 3.0 minimum grade point average. Undergraduate students enrolled full-time in a degree program at an accredited 2-year or 4-year college or universities are eligible to apply.

National Association of Black Accountants
7249 A Hanover Parkway
Greenbelt, MD 20770
www.nabainc.org

The National Association of Black Accountants awards student scholarships at both the national and local levels. Scholarships are awarded to deserving and successful college students to assist in furthering their education. The National Association of Black Accountants, Inc. (NABA) has provided more than $8 million in scholarship funds to deserving students preparing to enter various business professions. In 2009, the National Association of Black Accountants awarded close to $500,000. Scholarships of up to $10,000 are awarded to deserving students.

KPMG Foundation
Three Chestnut Ridge Road
Montvale, New Jersey 07645-0435
kpmgfoundation.org

The KPMG Foundation's Minority Accounting Doctoral Support Program awards renewable $10,000 annual scholarships to outstanding accounting students. The KPMG Foundation has awarded more than $8.7 million in scholarships to outstanding students.

U.S. Dept. of Energy-ORISE
www.orise.orau.gov
Oak Ridge Institute of Science and Energy (ORISE)
PO Box 117, Oak Ridge, TN 37831-0117

The Oak Ridge Institute of Science and Energy conducts annual summer internship for minority students, who are juniors, seniors and first year graduate students. Students, who major in Business Administration, Management, Finance, Accounting, Human Resources, Economics, Public Administration, or Computer Science, are eligible to apply. A Grade Point Average of 3.0 is required.

PNC Bank Scholarship Program
The United Negro Scholarship Fund
8260 Willow Oaks Corporate Drive
P.O. Box 10444, Fairfax, VA 22031
www.uncf.org

The PNC Bank Scholarship Program provides financial assistance to outstanding students majoring in business, accounting, economics, finance, marketing, mathematics, computer science, or information technology. Students who attend Morehouse, Clark Atlanta University, Florida A&M University, Hampton, Howard, Pennsylvania State University, Rutgers, Spelman College, Temple, or the University of Pittsburgh are eligible to participate.

BUSINESS SCHOLARSHIPS

NAACP EARL G. GRAVES SCHOLARSHIP

NAACP Education Department Scholarships
4805 Mt. Hope Drive
Baltimore, MD 21215-3297
www.naacp.org

The Earl G. Graves Scholarship provides financial assistance to students of Business Administration in their junior and senior year of their program. Graduate students of Business Administration are also eligible for assistance. Scholarships of $5,000 are awarded.

Ford Motors Scholars Program
The United Negro Scholarship Fund
8260 Willow Oaks Corporate Drive
P.O. Box 10444, Fairfax, VA 22031
www.uncf.org

The Ford Motors Scholars Program provides financial assistance to outstanding students majoring in Accounting, Computer Engineering, Electrical Engineering, Finance, Information Systems, Marketing, Mechanical Engineering, and Operations Management. The Ford Motors Scholars Program is also committed to providing a unique educational opportunity to students that participate. Scholarships of up to $5,000 are awarded to deserving students.

PNC Bank Scholarship Program
The United Negro Scholarship Fund
8260 Willow Oaks Corporate Drive
P.O. Box 10444, Fairfax, VA 22031
www.uncf.org

The PNC Bank Scholarship Program provides financial assistance to outstanding students majoring in business, accounting, economics, finance, marketing, mathematics, computer science, or information technology. Students who attend Morehouse College, Clark Atlanta University, Florida A&M University, Hampton University, Howard University, Pennsylvania State University, Rutgers University, Spelman College, Temple University, or the University of Pittsburgh are eligible to participate in this program.

Paine Webber Scholarships
The United Negro Scholarship Fund
8260 Willow Oaks Corporate Drive
P.O. Box 10444, Fairfax, VA 22031
www.uncf.org

The Paine Webber Scholarship Program, funded by a $500,000 endowment, provides renewable scholarships to UNCF students interested in business-related fields.

MasterCard Worldwide Scholars Program
The United Negro Scholarship Fund
8260 Willow Oaks Corporate Drive
P.O. Box 10444, Fairfax, VA 22031
www.uncf.org

The MasterCard Worldwide Scholars Program provides financial assistance to outstanding students majoring in Business, Finance, Accounting, Information Systems, and Marketing. The program is open to undergraduate students in their sophomore, and junior year. Students from all states are eligible to apply. The MasterCard Worldwide Scholars Program awards a $4,500 scholarship to defray the cost of tuition, fees, room and board.

Manor Care, Inc. Scholarship Program
The United Negro Scholarship Fund
8260 Willow Oaks Corporate Drive
P.O. Box 10444, Fairfax, VA 22031
www.uncf.org

Manor Care, Inc., through a $100,000 gift, provides scholarships to UNCF students pursuing degrees in business related fields, hotel and food service management, health care administration and human resources.

CBS Career Horizons Internship/Scholarship
The United Negro Scholarship Fund
8260 Willow Oaks Corporate Drive
P.O. Box 10444, Fairfax, VA 22031
www.uncf.org

This program is funded by a $250,000 grant from CBS Incorporated. It is open to sophomores and juniors enrolled at an historically black college or university with a minimum GPA of 3.0, majoring in accounting, business, finance, marketing, mass communications or journalism. Students participate in a summer internship; receive a $5,000 stipend and an $8,000 scholarship.

U.S. Dept. of Energy-ORISE
www.orise.orau.gov
Oak Ridge Institute of Science and Energy (ORISE)
PO Box 117
Oak Ridge, TN 37831-0117

The Oak Ridge Institute of Science and Energy conducts annual summer internship for minority students, who are juniors, seniors and first year graduate students. Students who major in Business Administration, Management, Finance, Accounting, Human Resources, Economics, Public Administration, Computer Science, or Instructional Technology are eligible to apply. A minimum Grade Point Average of 3.0 is required for eligibility. The internship is at the Oak Ridge Institute for Science and Education.

CHEMISTRY SCHOLARSHIPS

Chemists perform analytical research to determine the specific characteristics of different compounds and substances. Chemists use this information to create new materials, medicines, plastics, alloys and ceramics. There are approximately 94,100 chemists employed in government and industry in the United States. Today, if you eat it, clean with it, put it in your car, or feed it to your plants; it probably came from a chemist's lab. Chemists are in the business of researching the properties, composition, and principles of elements and compounds. Chemists apply basic chemical principles (like polymerization) to developing new products and processes. Chemists work in every sector, including academia, the private sector, and the government.

Median annual wages of chemists in May 2008 were $66,230. The middle 50 percent earned between $48,630 and $89,660. The highest 10 percent earned more than $113,080. According to the National Association of Colleges and Employers, beginning salary offers in July 2009 for graduates with a bachelor's degree in chemistry averaged $39,897 a year. In March 2009, annual earnings of chemists in nonsupervisory, supervisory, and managerial positions in the Federal Government averaged $101,687.

NAACP Willems Scholarship
Nat'l Assn for the Advancement of Colored People
NAACP Education Department
4805 Mt. Hope Drive
Baltimore, MD 21215-3297
www.naacp.org

The NAACP Willems Scholarship is awarded to male students who are majoring in Engineering, Chemistry, Physics, Computer and Mathematical Sciences. Applicants must possess a cumulative grade point average of at least 3.0 or B average, and must be members of the NAACP.

SOARS Program
University Corporation for Atmospheric Research
P.O. Box 3000, Boulder, CO 80307
www.soars.ucar.edu

The SOARS program provides financial assistance to students majoring in atmospheric science or a related field such as biology, chemistry, computer science, engineering, environmental science, mathematics, meteorology, oceanography, physics, or the social sciences. Students in their junior year from traditionally underrepresented groups in the atmospheric and related sciences are eligible to apply. Candidates should have a Grade Point Average of 3.0 or higher. Scholarships and stipends of $1500 to $2500 per month are awarded.

American Chemical Society
1155 16th Street, NW
Washington, DC 20036
www.acs.org

The American Chemical Society provides academic opportunities and financial support for outstanding chemistry students. To be considered as a candidate, a student must be a freshman, sophomore, and junior planning to complete a degree program in chemistry, biochemistry, or chemical engineering. Eligible students must also have a Grade Point Average of 3.0 or higher. Scholarships of $2500-$5000 are awarded to undergraduate students. Minority and economically disadvantaged high school students can also participate in a summer intern program run by the American Chemical Society.

William Wrigley, Jr. Company Scholars Program
The United Negro Scholarship Fund
8260 Willow Oaks Corporate Drive
P.O. Box 10444, Fairfax, VA 22031
www.uncf.org

The William Wrigley, Jr. Company Scholars Program, via a $250,000 endowment fund, provides financial assistance to seniors majoring in business, engineering or chemistry who attend a UNCF institution.

American Institute of Chemical Engineers
3 Park Avenue
New York, NY 10016
www.aiche.org

The American Institute of Chemical Engineers provides financial assistance to outstanding minority students who major in science, chemistry, or chemical engineering. Scholarship selections are based upon academic qualifications. Students are awarded scholarships of $1,000.

U.S. Air Force ROTC/Express Scholarship Program
HQ Air Force ROTC
551 E Maxwell Blvd
Maxwell AFB, AL 36112
www.afrotc.com/scholarships/in-college/express-scholarships/

The U.S. Air Force ROTC/Express Scholarship Program provides financial assistance to outstanding minority and exceptional non-minority college students, with 2-3 years remaining in education. A non-minority student must major in Computer Engineering, Computer Science, Meteorology, Math, Electrical Engineering, Nursing or Physics. Minority students may study any Bachelor Degree program.

Oak Ridge Associated Universities
Professional Internship Program in Fossil Energy
University Programs Division
P.O. Box 117, Oak Ridge, TN 37831
www.orau.org

The Oak Ridge Associated Universities Professional Internship Program in Fossil Energy provides research experience and financial support for students of engineering, the social, biological, and physical sciences. Graduate and undergraduate students in their sophomore year are eligible to apply. Participant selections are based upon academic qualifications. Interns receive $1,200 to $1,300 for up to 12 months.

CIVIL ENGINEERING SCHOLARSHIPS

There are more than 278,400 Civil engineers employed in the United States. Civil engineers build, repair, and design the infrastructure of the United States. Civil engineers build airports, bridges, highway exchanges, roads, water treatment facilities, waste disposal systems and reservoirs. Much of the infrastructure of the United States is aged and in need of repair or replacement. As a result, the demand for civil engineers will continue to grow as the United States rebuilds its' infrastructure. The need for Civil engineers is expected to grow 24 percent over the next decade. Demand is expected to grow by 67,600 positions or 345,900 jobs by 2018. The average yearly wages of Civil engineers were $78,560 in May 2008. The salary of the highest 10 percent of Civil engineers was more than $115,630.

National Society of Professional Engineers
NSPE Foundation Scholarships
1420 King Street, Alexandria, VA 22314
www.nspe.org

The NSPE Foundation offers scholarships to students who desire to pursue a career in engineering. NSPE Foundation offers financial assistance and academic enrichment activities to promising undergraduate students who plan to pursue a engineering degree. Renewable grants are available for undergraduate study.

National Action Council for Minorities in Engineering
440 Hamilton Ave, Suite 302
White Plains NY 10601
www.nacme.org

NACME provides financial assistance to minority students with financial need enrolled in a full-time undergraduate engineering program. NACME provides over $4,000,000 to 100 engineering schools.

AGC Scholarships
2300 Wilson Blvd., Suite 400
Arlington, VA 22201
www.agc.org

The Associated General Contractors of America has awarded more than $7.5 million to approximately 3,000 students attending 190 colleges and universities. The Associated General Contractors of America awards 100 or more scholarships each year. The AGC offers financial assistance outstanding students studying civil engineering or construction.

The American Society of Naval Engineers
1452 Duke Street
Alexandria, VA 22314
www.navalengineers.org

The American Society of Naval Engineers provides financial support to undergraduate and graduate engineering students. Undergraduate scholarships of up to $3,000 are available. Graduate students are eligible for awards of $4,000.

COMMUNICATIONS SCHOLARSHIPS

Digital transmission technology and cable television have dramatically changed the communications industry. Cable and satellite television broadcasting have opened new avenues for those seeking careers in broadcasting and electronic journalism. The proliferation of cable channels has created significant demand for programming and for those who have the skill to meet this demand. Minorities are underrepresented and undeserved by the communications industry. Newspapers, cable, public and broadcast television has renewed their efforts to encourage minorities to seek careers in journalism and communications.

A multitude of financial aid programs have been created to support African American students who seek careers in electronic communications and journalism.

Salaries for broadcast news analysts vary widely. Median annual wages of broadcast news analysts were $51,260 in May 2008. The highest 10 percent earned more than $156,200.

CBS Career Horizons Internship/Scholarship
The United Negro Scholarship Fund
8260 Willow Oaks Corporate Drive
P.O. Box 10444, Fairfax, VA 22031
www.uncf.org

This program is funded by a $250,000 grant from CBS Incorporated. It is open to sophomores and juniors enrolled at an historically black college or university with a minimum GPA of 3.0, majoring in accounting, business, finance, marketing, mass communications or journalism. Students participate in a summer internship; receive a $5,000 stipend and an $8,000 scholarship.

Ed Bradley Scholarship
Radio & News Television News Directors Foundation
529 14th Street, NW, Suite 425
Washington, D.C. 20045
www.rtdna.org

The Ed Bradley Scholarship provides financial assistance to minority full-time minority college students whose career objective is electronic journalism. Ed Bradley, the 60 Minutes correspondent at CBS News, was once a teacher and made a career switch to journalism. Mr. Bradley endowed this $10,000 annual award under the banner of the Radio & News Television News Directors Foundation.

George Foreman/Lyndon B. Johnson Scholarship
Radio & News Television News Directors Foundation
The National Press Building
529 14th Street, NW, Suite 425
Washington, D.C. 20045
www.rtdna.org

The George Foreman/ Lyndon B. Johnson Scholarship provides financial assistance to minority broadcast journalism students at the University of Texas at Austin. George Foreman a former heavy weight World Champion and Olympic Gold Medalist also enjoyed a long career as a television sports commentator. The former heavyweight champion, created this $6,000 annual scholarship to honor President Lyndon B. Johnson.

The Carole Simpson Scholarship
Radio & News Television News Directors Foundation
The National Press Building
529 14th Street, NW, Suite 425
Washington, D.C. 20045
www.rtdna.org

Carole Simpson, ABC news senior correspondent, created this annual $2,000 award to encourage and help minority students overcome hurdles along their career path.

National Public Radio
635 Massachusetts Avenue, NW,
Washington, DC 20001
internship@npr.org.

National Public Radio offers paid internships for students interested in careers in broadcasting. Students are also eligible for stipends awarded through the program in addition to intern pay.

The NPR Kroc Fellowship was established to identify and develop outstanding journalists for the public radio system. The NPR Kroc Fellowship is a one year program. A stipend of $40,000 is awarded. The NPR Kroc Fellowship was established through the generous $200 million contribution of Joan Kroc.

John Lennon Scholarship Fund
The United Negro Scholarship Fund
8260 Willow Oaks Corporate Drive
P.O. Box 10444, Fairfax, VA 22031
www.uncf.org

Yoko Ono created the John Lennon Scholarship Fund in memory of John Lennon. The income from this $800,000 endowment provides scholarships for UNCF students in the performing arts and communications. Scholarship amounts vary.

Rhythm Nation/Janet Jackson Scholarship
The United Negro Scholarship Fund
8260 Willow Oaks Corporate Drive
P.O. Box 10444, Fairfax, VA 22031
www.uncf.org

The Grammy Award winning artist Janet Jackson created this $395,000 endowed scholarship. Awards are made annually to students majoring in communications, music, performing arts, and the fine arts. Students must be enrolled in a UNCF college or university must demonstrate need, with a minimum 2.5 Grade Point Average. Inquiries must be made to the financial aid office at each school. Scholarship amounts vary.

Michael Jackson Endowed Scholarship Fund
The United Negro Scholarship Fund
8260 Willow Oaks Corporate Drive
P.O. Box 10444, Fairfax, VA 22031
www.uncf.org

Michael Jackson Scholarship for performing arts, funded by a $1.5 million endowment, provides renewable scholarships to UNCF students majoring in the performing arts, music, dance and communications. Students enrolled in a UNCF college or university, with demonstrated financial need, and a minimum 2.5 Grade Point Average are eligible.

COMPUTER SCIENCE SCHOLARSHIPS

Computers and Information Technology **(IT)** have become an integral part of modern life. Among its most important functions are the efficient transmission of information and the storage and analysis of information.

Overall employment of computer network, systems, and database administrators is projected to increase much faster than the average for all occupations over the next decade. More than 500,000 new (IT) jobs will be created from 2008-2018. Growth, however, will vary by specialty.

Median annual wages of network and computer systems administrators were $66,310 in May 2008. The highest 10 percent earned more than $104,070.

According to the National Association of Colleges and Employers, starting salary offers for graduates with a bachelor's degree in Information sciences averaged $55,084 a year in 2010.

Microsoft Scholarship Program
National Minority Technical Scholarship
Microsoft Corporation
One Microsoft Way
Redmond, WA 98052-8303
www.microsoft.com/college/scholarships

The Microsoft National Minority Technical Scholarship is awarded to outstanding students pursuing degrees in computer science, computer engineering, mathematics, and physics. Students are awarded full tuition scholarships. Students are also provided 12 week paid internships with Microsoft.

Blacks at Microsoft Scholarships
Microsoft Corporation
One Microsoft Way
Redmond, WA 98052-8303
www.microsoft.com/college/scholarships

The Blacks at Microsoft Scholarships program provides financial assistance to outstanding students pursuing a degree in computer science, engineering, finance, business administration and marketing. To be eligible, students must have a 3.30 minimum grade point average. Scholarships are awarded to outstanding students who have a passion for technology. The scholarships are renewable for 4 years.

Xerox Technical Minority Scholarship Program
150 State Street, 4th Floor
Rochester, NY 14614
www.xeroxstudentcareers.com

The Xerox Technical Minority Scholarship Program provides financial assistance to outstanding students pursuing a degree in Chemistry, Information Management, Physics, and Computer Engineering, Electrical Engineering, and Chemical Engineering Eligible, students must have a 3.00 GPA. Scholarships are awarded to outstanding students who have a passion for technology. The scholarships of up to $10,000 are awarded.

The National GEM Consortium
1430 Duke Street
Alexandria, VA 22314
www.gemfellowship.org

MS Engineering Fellowship Program

The MS Engineering Fellowship Program provides financial assistance to engineering students in order to promote the benefits of obtaining a masters degree in engineering. The Fellowship provides full tuition, fees and a stipend of $10,000. The Fellowship includes 2 summers of paid internships. The stipend may be used at any participating GEM University where the student has been admitted.

Ph.D. Engineering Fellowship Program

The Ph.D. Engineering Fellowship Program provides financial assistance to minority students who have completed or are enrolled in a Masters Degree program. The GEM Consortium provides the first years funding for tuition and fees. A Stipend of $14,000 is provided. The Fellowship provides a paid summer internship

Ph.D. Science Fellowship Program

The goal of the Ph.D. Science Fellowship Program is to increase the number of minority students who pursue doctoral degrees in the natural science, chemistry, physics, earth sciences, mathematics, biological sciences, and computer science. Students who are enrolled in a Masters Degree program are eligible to apply. Students can apply and be accepted in the program as early as their junior undergraduate year. Tuition and fees are waived for Ph.D. Science Fellowship Program students. Students receive a 1 year stipend of $14,000. The Fellowship program provides a paid summer internship.

Louis Stokes Science and Technology Award
NAACP Education Department
4805 Mt. Hope Drive, Baltimore, MD 21215
www.naacp.org

The NAACP/Louis Stokes Science and Technology award provides scholarships for incoming freshman that major in engineering, science, computer science or mathematical science.

U.S. Dept. of Energy-ORISE
Oak Ridge Institute of Science and Energy (ORISE)
PO Box 117, Oak Ridge, TN 37831
www.orise.orau.gov

The Oak Ridge Institute of Science and Energy conducts Annual summer internship for minority students, who are juniors, seniors and first year graduate students, studying Business Administration, Management, Finance, Accounting, Human Resources, Economics, Public Administration, Computer Science, or Instructional Technology. A Grade Point Average of 3.0 is required for eligibility.

U.S. Air Force ROTC/Express Scholarship Program
551 E Maxwell Blvd
Maxwell AFB, AL 36112
www.afrotc.com/scholarships

The U.S. Air Force ROTC/Express Scholarship Program provides financial assistance to outstanding minority and exceptional non-minority college students, with 2-3 years remaining in education. A non-minority student must major in Computer Engineering, Computer Science, Meteorology, Math, Electrical Engineering, Nursing or Physics. Minority students may study any Bachelor Degree program.

ECONOMICS SCHOLARSHIPS

Economics is how a society allocates its scarce resources. The globalization of the world economy has intensified the need for strategic economic planning and decision making, thereby increasing the demand for economists and other business policy makers. The median salary of all economists in 2008 was $83,590. The average salary for economists in government employ in 2009 was $108,010 per year. The highest 10 percent earned more than $149,100.

American Economic Association
2014 Broadway, Suite 305
Nashville, TN 37203
(615) 322-2595

The American Economic Association's Summer Program and Minority Scholarship Program offers financial assistance and academic enrichment activities to promising undergraduate students who plan to pursue a doctoral degree. Graduate level economic course work is exposed to the institute participants during the program. The full cost of the institute and a stipend is awarded. The American Economic Association's Summer Program is now based at the University of California Santa Barbara.

National Economics Association
Summer Economics Fellows Program
Kentucky State University, School of Business
Frankfort, KY 40601
www.neaecon.org

Summer Economics Fellows Program is sponsored in part by the National Science Foundation. The purpose of the Summer Economics Fellows Program is to increase the participation of women and underrepresented minorities in economics. The fellowship allows students of superior academic ability to spend a summer in residence at a sponsoring research institution. Graduate and Doctoral students of economics are eligible to apply. Students are compensated within the guidelines of the participating research organizations. Participating sponsors include organizations like the; The Board of Governors of the Federal Reserve, the Brookings Institution, the Bureau of Economic Analysis, the Bureau of Labor Statistics, the Census Bureau, the International Monetary Fund, the Rand Corporation, the Federal Reserve Bank of Atlanta, the Environmental Protection Agency, the Economic Research Service, the Federal Reserve Bank of San Francisco, Microsoft, the Federal Reserve Bank of Atlanta, and the Urban Institute.

U.S. Department of Education
Jacob K. Javits Fellowship Program
400 Maryland Avenue, SW
Washington, DC 20202
www2.ed.gov/programs/jacobjavits/index

The Jacob K. Javits Fellowship Program provides financial support for graduate students, graduating college seniors of the social sciences. The Jacob K. Javits Fellowship Program provides fellowships to students of superior academic ability. Jacob K. Javits Fellows are selected on the basis of demonstrated achievement, financial need, and exceptional promise. Doctoral students majoring in the social sciences and humanities are eligible to apply Fellowships are for up to 48 months or the completion of the degree. A stipend of up to $30,000 is awarded.

Scholars Program
Harvard University Ctr. of International Affairs
www.wcfia.harvard.edu
1737 Cambridge Street
Cambridge, MA 02138

The Harvard Academy for International and Area Studies Scholars Program provides financial support for doctoral candidates of economics, political science, and law. Awards are based upon academic achievement and the proposed research. The program awards grants of $22,000 to $36,000 for 2 years.

PNC Bank Scholarship Program
THE UNITED NEGRO SCHOLARSHIP FUND
8260 Willow Oaks Corporate Drive
P.O. Box 10444, Fairfax, VA 22031-4511
www.uncf.org

The PNC Bank Scholarship Program provides financial assistance to outstanding students majoring in business, accounting, economics, finance, marketing, mathematics, computer science, or information technology. A minimum grade point average of 3.0 is required for eligibility. Students who attend Morehouse College, Clark Atlanta University, Florida A&M University, Hampton University, Howard University, Pennsylvania State University, Rutgers University, Spelman College, Temple University, or the University of Pittsburgh are eligible to participate.

U.S. Dept. of Energy-ORISE
www.orise.orau.gov
Oak Ridge Institute of Science and Energy
PO Box 117, Oak Ridge, TN 37831

The Oak Ridge Institute of Science and Energy conducts annual summer internship for minority students, who are juniors, seniors and first year graduate students. Students who major in Business Administration, Management, Finance, Accounting,

Human Resources, Economics, Public Administration, Computer Science, or Instructional Technology are eligible to apply. A minimum Grade Point Average of 3.0 is required for eligibility. The internship is at the Oak Ridge Institute for Science and Education. Student awards are based on the educational level completed. Students are provided with a weekly stipend and reimbursement for travel.

National Urban Fellows

National Urban Fellows
102 West 38th Street, Suite 700
New York, NY 10018
www.nuf.org

The National Urban Fellows Program provides financial assistance to outstanding minority students of Urban Administration. The National Urban Fellows participate in a full-time graduate degree program. Two semesters of academic course work and a nine-month mentorship assignment are required. Upon completion, National Urban Fellows are awarded the Master of Public Administration (MPA) degree from the City of New York's Bernard M. Baruch College, School of Public Affairs. The National Urban Fellows Program includes full tuition and fees, health insurance, a book allowance and $25,000 stipend. Relocation and travel expenses are reimbursed.

EDUCATION SCHOLARSHIPS

Education is the nations' largest sector of employment. There are 3,476,200 million people working as teachers in the nation's schools. Teachers complete a 4 year Bachelor of Arts program in education. Students who complete the bachelor's degree in another field can become certified by completing specific course requirements in some states. Over the next decade, 468,000 new teachers will be needed by 2018.

Teacher pay varies by municipality. Teacher salaries nationwide average $33,227 for first year educators. The median annual wages of kindergarten, elementary, middle, and secondary school teachers ranged from $47,100 to $51,180 in May 2008; the top 10 percent earned $75,190 to $80,970.

College & University Faculty

There are more than 1,699,200 people teaching in our nation's colleges and universities.
Retirements and an increase in the percentage of students who will attend college will ensure strong demand for college and university faculty through the year 2018. Over the next decade the number should rise to 1,956,100 by 2018.

The median annual earnings of all postsecondary teachers in May 2008 were $58,830. The middle 50 percent earned between $41,600 and $83,960. The highest 10 percent earned more than $121,850.

Earnings for college faculty vary with the rank and type of institution, geographic area, and field. According to a 2008–09 survey by the American Association of University Professors, salaries for full-time faculty averaged $79,439. By rank, the average was $108,749 for professors, $76,147 for associate professors, and $63,827 for assistant professors.

Mellon Mays Undergraduate Fellowship Program
The Andrew W. Mellon Foundation
140 East 62nd Street
New York, NY 10065
www.mmuf.org

The Mellon Mays Undergraduate Fellowship (MMUF) promotes the increase of college faculty of color. The program supports outstanding minority students who are pursuing PhDs in the arts and sciences. The MMUF program has had over 3,200 participating students. More than 290 students have earned their PhD. There are 550 other candidates working toward their PhD. The program honors Dr. Benjamin E. Mays, the noted African-American educator, minister, and former president of Morehouse College. At Morehouse College Dr. Mays became a mentor to Dr. Martin Luther King, Jr.

McKnight Black Doctoral Fellowship Program
The Florida Education Fund
201 East Kennedy Boulevard, Suite 1525
Tampa, Florida 33602
mdf@fefonline.org

The McKnight Black Doctoral Fellowship Program supports outstanding minority students who are pursuing PhDs in Business Administration, Computer Science, Biology, Marine Biology, Engineering, Mathematics, Chemistry, Physics and Psychology.

The McKnight Black Doctoral Fellowship Program awards $17,000 per year in tuition and fees. A stipend of $12,000 is awarded to fellows. The program provides comprehensive academic support to participants. The Fellowship is renewable for 5 years with satisfactory academic progress.

The McKnight Black Doctoral Fellowship Program has awarded approximately 700 Fellowships. More than 274 Fellows have graduated with the Ph.D. degree, within five years. The McKnight Black Doctoral Fellowship Program has an 80% retention rate. Each year the McKnight Black Doctoral Fellowship Program awards up to 50 fellowships to outstanding students. Florida Agricultural and Mechanical University and the University of Miami are two of the colleges that participate in the McKnight Black Doctoral Fellowship Program.

Howard University
2400 Sixth Street NW
Washington DC 20059
www.howard.edu

The Frederick Douglass Scholars Program provides up to $75,000 in stipend support, full tuition, and research funding, for students who wish to pursue college or university teaching as a career. Frederick Douglass Scholars are required to maintain a 3.50 minimum grade point average.

TEACH Grant Program
U.S. Department of Education
400 Maryland Avenue, SW
Washington, DC 20202-5251
www2.ed.gov
The TEACH Grant is available to eligible students who agree teach in low income areas. The grant is available to who agree to teach in a public or private elementary or secondary school that serves students from low-income families. Students who major in Mathematics, Science, Bilingual Education and English Language Acquisition and Special Education are eligible to participate in the TEACH Grant Program. Undergraduate and graduate students are eligible. A 3.0 grade point average is necessary for consideration. The TEACH Grant program awards $4,000 to deserving students. Students must maintain their academic performance to renew the grant for the second year.

ENGINEERING AND SCIENCE SCHOLARSHIPS

America's economic future is dependent on its ability to maintain and expand its technological expertise. African Americans are disproportionally underrepresented in the fields of science and engineering. The Federal Government, the Fortune 500, and academia have renewed their efforts to encourage minorities to seek careers in science. A multitude of financial aid programs have been established to help African American students who seek careers in engineering and science. There are more than 1,571,900 Engineers in the United States. The field will grow to more than 1,750,300 engineers by 2018.

Mickey Leland Energy Fellowship

U.S. Department of Energy
19901 Germantown Rd.
Germantown, MD 20874
www.science.gov

The Mickey Leland Energy Fellowship is a 10 week summer internship program sponsored by the U.S. Department of Energy's Office of Fossil Energy. Outstanding minority and women students are eligible to apply. The Mickey Leland Energy Fellowship provides a $5,000 stipend to undergraduate pursuing degrees in mathematics, science, engineering and technology. Graduate students are awarded a stipend of $6,500.

Fannie and John Hertz Foundation
2456 Research Drive
Livermore, CA 94550-3850
www.hertzfoundation.org

The Hertz Foundation provides financial assistance to graduate students working towards the Ph.D. degree in the applied physical, biological and engineering sciences. The Hertz Fellowship Program includes full tuition and fees and $31,000 stipend. The Hertz Foundation Fellowship is renewable for 5 years.

The Society of Women Engineers
120 S La Salle Street, Suite 1515
Chicago, IL 60603
www.societyofwomenengineers.swe.org

The Society of Women Engineers Scholarship Program provides financial assistance to women in baccalaureate or graduate programs, who are pursuing careers in engineering, engineering technology and computer science. The Society of Women Engineers awarded more than $470,000 in scholarships in 2009.

American Institute of Aeronautics and Astronautics
AIAA Foundation Scholarships
1801 Alexander Bell Drive, Suite 500
Reston, VA 20191-4344
www.aiaa.org

The American Institute of Aeronautics and Astronautics Foundation (AIAA) provides financial assistance to undergraduate students pursuing careers in the aerospace industry. Scholarships of $2,000 - $2,500 are awarded to outstanding undergraduate students who major in engineering, science, and aerospace engineering. AIAA Foundation Scholarships are renewable for 4 years for undergraduate students.

The AIAA Foundation Scholarships program provides financial assistance to graduate students as well. Scholarships of $5,000 - $10,000 are awarded to outstanding graduate-level students.

The Paul H. Robbins, P.E., Honorary Scholarship
National Society of Professional Engineers
1420 King Street, Alexandria, VA 22314
www.nspe.org

The Paul H. Robbins, P.E., Honorary Scholarship is awarded to an engineering student at an accredited program. Engineering students entering their junior year are eligible to apply. Scholarships of $5,000 are awarded.

Steinman Scholarship Award
National Society of Professional Engineers
1420 King Street, Alexandria, VA 22314
www.nspe.org

The Steinman Scholarship is awarded to outstanding undergraduates students pursuing a degree in engineering. Students entering their junior are eligible to participate in this program. Scholarships in the amount of $5,000 are awarded.

Maureen and Howard Blitman Scholarship
National Society of Professional Engineers
1420 King Street, Alexandria, VA 22314
www.nspe.org

The Maureen L. and Howard N. Blitman Scholarship program is designed to promote diversity in engineering. Outstanding minority students who have been accepted into an accredited engineering program are eligible to apply. Scholarships totaling $5,000 are awarded in 2 installments.

National Radio Astronomy Observatory
Summer Student Program
520 Edgemont Road
Charlottesville, VA 22903-2475
www.science.nrao.edu

The National Radio Astronomy Observatory Summer Student Program is a paid 10 week summer internship program. The NRA Observatory Summer Student Program provides work experience and financial assistance to graduate and undergraduate students of physics, computer sciences, electrical engineering and astronomy. The National Radio Astronomy Observatory Summer Student Program provides a $5,920 stipend to undergraduate students. Graduate students are awarded a stipend of $6,340.

The American Physics Society
The American Physics Society Minority Scholarship
American Center for Physics
One Physics Ellipse
College Park, MD 20740
www.aps.org

The American Physics Society provides financial assistance to undergraduate minority physics students. African American, Hispanic, or Native Americans enrolled in universities with predominate minority enrollments are eligible. Scholarships are provided for tuition, room, and board. The American Physics Society has awarded scholarships to more than 250 outstanding students.

Argonne National Laboratory
U.S. Department of Energy
Science Undergraduate Laboratory Internships
9700 South Cass Avenue, Argonne, IL 60439
www.dep.anl.gov

The U.S. Department of Energy's Science Undergraduate Laboratory Internships Program is a paid 10 week summer internship program. Outstanding full-time undergraduate students are eligible to apply. To be eligible, students must have a 2.5 minimum grade point average. The Science Undergraduate Laboratory Internships Program provides a $4,250 stipend to undergraduate pursuing degrees in mathematics, science, engineering and technology. Travel expenses are reimbursed.

U.S. Dept. of Energy-ORISE
www.orise.orau.gov
Oak Ridge Institute of Science and Energy
PO Box 117, Oak Ridge, TN 37831

The Oak Ridge Institute of Science and Energy conducts annual summer internship for minority students, who are juniors, seniors and first year graduate students. Students who major in Business Administration, Management, Finance, Accounting, Human Resources, Economics, Public Administration, Computer Science, or Instructional Technology are eligible to apply. A minimum Grade Point Average of 3.0 is required for eligibility. The internship is at the Oak Ridge Institute for Science and Education. Student awards are based on the educational level completed. Students are provided with a weekly stipend and reimbursement for travel.

LAW SCHOLARSHIPS

Thurgood Marshall
B.A. Lincoln University, JD Howard University
Supreme Court Justice emeritus

Thurgood Marshall earned his bachelors' degree at Lincoln University. Denied admission to the University of Maryland Law School because of his race, Marshall continued his studies as a magna cum laude graduate of Howard University Law School in 1933. In one of his first cases he chose to represent Donald Murray. Donald Murray had also been denied admission into the University of Maryland Law School because of his race. Marshall won that case and went on to win 29 of 32 cases he brought before the Supreme Court of the United States.

Today, there are more than 759,200 lawyers working in the United States. Candidates for admission to law school must possess the Bachelors degree to be considered. After completing Law school the student receives the JD (Juris Doctor) or the LLM degree.

The demand for new lawyers is expected to grow by 98,500 positions or 857,700 jobs over the next decade. Job growth for lawyers will result from the increasing demand for legal services in such areas as healthcare, intellectual property, bankruptcy, corporate and security litigation, antitrust law, and environmental law.

In May 2008, the median annual wages of all wage-and-salaried lawyers were $110,590. The middle half of the occupation earned between $74,980 and $163,320.

African American Law Schools

Howard University School of Law
2900 Van Ness Street
Washington, DC 20008
www.law.howard.edu

Florida A&M University College of Law
One N. Orange Ave.
Orlando, Fl, 32801
407-254-3268

Thurgood Marshall School of Law
Texas Southern University
3100 Cleburne Street
Houston, Texas 77004
www.tsulaw.edu

North Carolina Central Law Center
1512 S. Alston Avenue
Durham, NC 27707
www.nccu.edu/law

Southern University Law Center
P.O. Box 9294, Baton Rouge, LA 70813
www.sulc.sus.edu

Council on Legal Education Opportunity
Thurgood Marshall
Legal Educational Opportunity Program
740 15th Street, NW 9th Floor
Washington DC 20005
866-886-4343
cleo@abanet.org

The Legal Education Opportunity Program provides economically disadvantaged students with the opportunity to attend law school. Minority students are a major focus of the program. Participants attend legal education summer institutes where necessary skills for the successful completion of legal study are imparted. Partial tuition scholarships are available on a limited basis. Participating law schools also provide variety of financial aids such as; tuition waivers, grants, and loans.

Raymond W. Cannon Memorial Scholarship
The United Negro Scholarship Fund
8260 Willow Oaks Corporate Drive
P.O. Box 10444, Fairfax, VA 22031
www.uncf.org

The Raymond W. Cannon Memorial Scholarship Program provides financial assistance through a $500,000 endowment fund established by Raymond W. Cannon. Scholarships are awarded annually to UNCF students majoring in pharmacy or pre-law and who have demonstrated leadership in high school and college.

The Earl Warren Legal Training Program
99 Hudson Street, Suite 1600
New York, NY 10013
www.naacplpf.org/scholarships

The Earl Warren Legal Training Program seeks to increase the number of African American lawyers in the United States. The program is supported by the NAACP Legal Defense and Educational Fund. The Earl Warren Legal Training Program awards three-year scholarships to outstanding law students. The Earl Warren Legal Training Program has awarded more than $10 million in financial support to undergraduate and law students.

American Bar Association
Legal Opportunity Scholarship Fund
321 North Clark Street
Chicago, Illinois 60654
abanet.org

The American Bar Association's Legal Opportunity Scholarship Fund provides financial assistance to outstanding law students. Students are able to use their scholarship funds at any ABA-accredited law school. Scholarships of up to $15,000 are awarded to students that qualify. In many cases, ABA Legal Opportunity Scholars are awarded matching grants by their law schools.

Summer Research Fellowships
Minority Undergraduates

American Bar Foundation
750 N. Lake Shore Drive, Chicago, IL 60611
fellowships@abfn.org

The American Bar Foundation Summer Research Fellowships for Minority Undergraduates provide financial assistance and academic enrichment opportunities for prospective law students. Minority students in their sophomore and junior years with a minimum 3.0 GPA are eligible to apply. Summer Research Fellowships will work at the American Bar Foundation's offices in Chicago, Illinois. Summer Research Fellows will receive a stipend during the program.

BESLA

Black Entertainment & Sports Lawyers Assoc
709-A 8th Street SE
Washington, DC 20003

The Black Entertainment & Sports Lawyers Association provides financial assistance to African American law students that attend Howard University Law School, North Carolina Central Law School, Southern University Law School or Texas Southern University Thurgood Marshall Law School. Eligible students should have taken an entertainment law or sports law related course, or actively participated in the entertainment or sports law field through internship or job. Students that have attended an entertainment law or sports law seminar or conference since commencing law school are also eligible. BESLA also administers the following programs; the Jack & Sayde B. Gibson Scholarship Fund, the Malena Rance Scholarship Fund, the LeBaron & Yvonne Taylor Scholarship Fund, and the BESLA/Budweiser Urban Scholarship Fund.

National Bar Association
1225 11th Street, NW Washington, D.C. 20001
www.nationalbar.org
(202) 842-3900

The National Bar Association was established in 1925 after Gertrude Rush, George H. Woodson, S. Joe Brown, James B. Morris, and Charles P. Howard, Sr. were denied membership in the American Bar Association. The National Bar Association represents the interests of African-American attorneys in the United States. The association has several affiliate chapters located throughout the United States. The National Bar Association provides program assistance and guidance to future attorneys. The National Bar Association administers a number of programs to help convey the importance of the legal profession to the African American community.

MBA SCHOLARSHIPS

Management Consultants evaluate financial statements, employee productivity, market movements, and the firm's financial commitments in order to make recommendations that will ensure the profitable operation of a business. Management analysts are often referred to as *management consultants* in private industry. Management Consultant salaries vary widely. Experience, education, area of expertise, and the size of the employer factor into compensation. Management Consultants employed in large firms or in major metropolitan areas have the highest salaries. The median annual wages of Management Consultants were $73,570 in May 2008. The salary of the highest 10 percent of Management Consultants was more than $133,850.

There are more than 746,900 Management Consultants employed in the United States. Employment demand for management analysts is expected to grow by 24 percent over the next decade. Demand is expected to grow by 178,300 positions or 925,200 jobs by 2018. Job growth is projected in large international consulting organizations and firms with expertise in healthcare, information technology, marketing, engineering, and biotechnology.

National Black MBA Association, Inc.
180 N. Michigan Ave., Suite 1400
Chicago, IL 60601
www.nbmbaa.org

The National Black MBA Association provides financial assistance to African American graduate business students. The National Black MBA Association has awarded more than $5 Million since the beginning of the program. Each year the National Black MBA Association awards more than $500,000 to outstanding students. Scholarships of up to $15,000 are awarded. The National Black MBA Association also offers financial assistance to undergraduate and Doctoral students.

Earl G. Graves Scholarship
NAACP Education Department Scholarships
4805 Mt. Hope Drive
Baltimore, MD 21215
www.naacp.org

The Earl G. Graves Scholarship provides financial assistance to students of Business Administration in their junior and senior year of their program. Graduate students of Business Administration are also eligible for assistance. Scholarships of up to $5,000 are awarded.

Government Finance Officers Association
Minorities in Government Finance Scholarship
180 North Michigan Avenue, Suite 800
Chicago, IL 60601-7476
www.gfoa.org

The Government Finance Officers Association provides financial assistance to full or part-time upper-division undergraduate or graduate students. Students of public administration, governmental accounting finance, political science, economics or business administration, and who plan to pursue a career in state or local government finance are eligible. Scholarships of $5,000 are awarded.

The Consortium
5585 Pershing Avenue, Suite 240
St. Louis, MO 63112
(888) 658-6814
www.cgsm.org

The Consortium for Graduate Study in Management provides financial assistance to outstanding graduate business students. The Consortium awards more than 350 fellowships each year.

U.S. Dept. of Energy-ORISE
Oak Ridge Institute of Science and Energy (ORISE)
PO Box 117, Oak Ridge, TN 37831
www.orise.orau.gov

The Oak Ridge Institute of Science and Energy conducts annual summer internship for minority students, who are juniors, seniors and first year graduate students, studying in Business Administration, Management, Finance, Accounting, Human Resources, Economics, Public Administration, Computer Science, Information Technology, Physics, Mathematics, and Statistics. A minimum Grade Point Average of 3.0 is required for eligibility. The internship is at the Oak Ridge Institute for Science and Education. Awards are based on educational level completed ($335 to $420 per week) and travel reimbursements are provided. The number of awards may vary.

American Planning Association
205 N. Michigan Ave., Suite 1200
Chicago, IL 60601
www.planning.org/scholarships/apa/

The American Planning Association provides financial assistance to outstanding graduate students who are candidates for the master's degree in planning.

National Urban Fellows

National Urban Fellows
102 West 38th Street, Suite 700
New York, NY 10018
www.nuf.org

The National Urban Fellows Program provides financial assistance to outstanding minority students of Urban Administration. The National Urban Fellows participate in a full-time graduate degree program. Two semesters of academic course work and a nine-month mentorship assignment are required. Upon completion, National Urban Fellows are awarded the Master of Public Administration (MPA) degree from the City of New York's Bernard M. Baruch College, School of Public Affairs. The National Urban Fellows Program includes full tuition and fees, health insurance, a book allowance and $25,000 stipend. Relocation and travel expenses are reimbursed.

MEDICAL SCHOLARSHIPS

The healthcare and medical professions are the nation's second largest area of employment. The United States spends more on health care than any other nation. The population of United States continues to expand and age. Healthcare expenditures will increase proportionally. Employment in the healthcare sector will continue to increase. There are more than 661,400 physicians employed in the United States. Demand is expected to grow by 144,100 positions or 805,500 jobs by 2018.

African Americans are underrepresented as health care providers and as the recipients of healthcare services. There are many financial aid programs that seek to encourage African Americans to pursue careers in the medical professions. These financial aid programs also promote specialty study. Physicians are people who have earned their M.D. (Doctors of Medicine) or the D.O. (Doctors of Osteopathy) Degree. To be considered for medical school, candidates must hold the bachelors degree in an appropriate field. Most physicians attend medical school over 4 years. Upon completing medical school, most Medical Doctors (M.D) begin a graduate residency program of 3 to 8 years depending on the specialty chosen. The time commitment that is necessary to become a physician is substantial. The personal and financial rewards last a lifetime. Physicians averaged $186,044 in salary in 2008. Specialists averaged $339,738 in salary in 2008.

National Health Service Corps
5600 Fishers Lane
Rockville, MD
800-221-9393
www.nhsc.hrsa.gov/scholarship

The National Health Service Corps scholarship pays tuition, required fees, and some other education costs, tax free, for as many as four years. Education costs may include books, clinical supplies, laboratory expenses, instruments, two sets of uniforms and travel for one clinical rotation. Students pursuing a Medical Degree (MD or DO) are eligible to participate. National Health Service Corps scholars receive a living stipend of up to $15,468 ($1,289 per month). National Health Service Corps scholars are committed to serve one year for each year of financial support received. A minimum commitment of two years of service is required.

Maryland Higher Education Commission
Graduate and Professional Scholarships
839 Bestgate Road, Suite 400
Annapolis, MD 21401
410-260-4500
www.mhec.state.md.us/financialaid

The Maryland Higher Education Commission Graduate and Professional Scholarship Program provides financial assistance to Maryland residents who are pursuing programs in medicine, dentistry, law, nursing, pharmacy, social work, and veterinary medicine. Scholarships of up to $5,000 are awarded.

National Medical Association
8403 Colesville Road, Suite 920
Silver Spring, Maryland 20910
www.nmanet.org
202-347-1895

The NMA seeks to encourage African American students to enter into medical training. Scholarships and loans are provided to qualified minority students accepted and enrolled in accredited medical schools.

Student National Medical Association
5113 Georgia Ave NW
Washington DC 20011
www.snma.org
202-882-2881

The Student National Medical Association was established in 1964 by medical students from Howard University College of Medicine and Meharry Medical College. The SNMA is the nation's oldest and largest independent, student-run organization focused on the needs and concerns of medical students of color. More than 8,000 medical students, pre-medical students, residents and physicians are members of the SNMA. The SNMA promotes and supports a number of programs to assist medical students.

NURSING SCHOLARSHIPS

There are more than 2.6 million nurses employed in the United States. Registered Nurses (RN's) and Licensed Nurse Practitioners (LPN's) receive their training at accredited 2 or 4 year colleges and universities. Demand is expected to grow by 580,000 positions or 3,200,000 jobs over the next decade

Registered Nurses (RN's) and Licensed Nurse Practitioners (LPN's) are also required to complete a program of classroom and supervised practice in an approved teaching hospital or medical facility. The demand for qualified nurses continues to grow and salaries are reflective of the growing reliance on nurses to provide elementary diagnostic services. The median annual wages of registered nurses were $62,450 in May 2008. The salary of the highest 10 percent of registered nurses was more than $92,240.

National Student Nurses Association
Undergraduate Scholarship Program
45 Main Street, Suite 606
Brooklyn, NY 11201
www.nsna.org

The Foundation of the National Student Nurses' Association Undergraduate Scholarship Program seeks to encourage outstanding students to consider nursing as a career. Practicing nurses provide guidance on entering the nursing profession. Over $125,000 in financial assistance is available each year. Scholarships range from $1,000 to $2,500.

Nursing Scholarship Program
Health Resources Service Administration
12530 Parklawn Drive, Suite 350
Rockville, MD 20852
800-221-9393
www.hrsa.gov

The Nursing Scholarship Program provides financial assistance to outstanding nursing students. The goal of the Nursing Scholarship Program is to help alleviate the critical shortage of registered nurses in the United States. The Nursing Scholarship Program includes full tuition and fees. A monthly stipend $1,326 is provided to students to help defray living expenses. A payment of $1,931 is provided for other reasonable educational expenses.

National Health Service Corps
5600 Fishers Lane
Rockville, MD
800-221-9393
www.nhsc.hrsa.gov/scholarship

The National Health Service Corps scholarship pays tuition, required fees, and some other education costs, tax free, for as many as four years. Students pursuing a Master Degree as a Family Nurse Practitioner are eligible to participate. National Health Service Corps scholars receive a living stipend of up to $15,468. National Health Service Corps scholars are committed to serve one year for each year of financial support received. A minimum commitment of two years of service is required.

PHARMACY SCHOLARSHIPS

Pharmacists held about 269,000 jobs in 2008. Employment is expected to grow to 315,000 by 2018.

The American Council on Pharmaceutical Education accredits colleges of pharmacy to confer degrees. Pharmacy programs grant the degree of Doctor of Pharmacy (Pharm.D.), which requires at least 6 years of postsecondary study and the passing of the licensure examination of a State board of pharmacy.

The Pharm.D is a 4-year program that requires at least 2 years of college study prior to admittance. This degree has replaced the Bachelor of Science (BS) degree.

The median annual salary of pharmacists in their first year of practice was between $82,356. The median annual wages of wage and salary pharmacists in May 2008 were $106,410. The middle 50 percent earned between $92,670 and $121,310 a year. The highest 10 percent earned more than $131,440 a year.

UNCF/ Metropolitan Life Scholarship Program
The United Negro Scholarship Fund
8260 Willow Oaks Corporate Drive
P.O. Box 10444, Fairfax, VA 22031
www.uncf.org

The Metropolitan Life Scholarship Program was created with a gift of $500,000 from the Metropolitan Life Insurance Company. The Metropolitan Life Scholarship Program provides financial and technical assistance UNCF juniors and seniors majoring in teacher education and health-related fields. Awards are made annually to students majoring in communications, music, performing arts, and the fine arts. Students must be enrolled in a UNCF college or university must demonstrate need, with a minimum 2.5 Grade Point Average. Inquiries must be made to the financial aid office at each school. Scholarship amounts vary.

UNCF/Revlon Women's Health Scholars Program
The United Negro Scholarship Fund
8260 Willow Oaks Corporate Drive
P.O. Box 10444, Fairfax, VA 22031
www.uncf.org

The Revlon Women's Health Scholars Program, established with a grant of $500,000, will provide annual scholarships of up to $10,000 to female UNCF students in their junior year pursuing degrees in pre-medicine or other healthcare related fields. Interested students must maintain a minimum 3.0 GPA and show excellent interpersonal skills and leadership abilities.

Raymond W. Cannon Memorial Scholarship
The United Negro Scholarship Fund
8260 Willow Oaks Corporate Drive
P.O. Box 10444, Fairfax, VA 22031
www.uncf.org

The Raymond W. Cannon Memorial Scholarship Program provides financial assistance through a $500,000 endowment fund established by Raymond W. Cannon. Scholarships are awarded annually to UNCF students majoring in pharmacy or pre-law and who have demonstrated leadership in high school and college.

Rite Aid/UNCF Retail Pharmacy Scholars Program
The United Negro Scholarship Fund
8260 Willow Oaks Corporate Drive
P.O. Box 10444, Fairfax, VA 22031
www.uncf.org

The Rite Aid/UNCF Retail Pharmacy Scholars Program was established in 1999. The Rite Aid/UNCF Retail Pharmacy Scholars Program offers a total of $25,000 in scholarships annually to pharmacy students attending Historically Black Colleges and Universities. Scholarships of up to $2,500 per student are awarded to those who qualify.

National Assoc. of Chain Drug Stores Foundation
NACDS Foundation Pharmacy Partners Scholarship
NACDS Foundation
413 N. Lee Street
Alexandria, VA 22314
www.nacdsfoundation.org

The goal of the NACDS Foundation Pharmacy Student Scholarship Program is to support the development of future leaders in chain drug stores and community pharmacies. Scholarships of $2,000 to $20,000 are awarded to outstanding students.

American Foundation for Pharmaceutical Education
Radburn Plaza Bldg., 14-25 Plaza Road
Fair Lawn, NJ 07410
www.afpenet.org

The American Foundation for Pharmaceutical Education provides financial assistance to graduate students of pharmaceutical sciences. Fellowships of $5,000-$7,000 are available.

National Pharmaceutical Foundation, Inc.
1728 17th, NW
Washington, DC 20002
www.snpha.org

The National Pharmaceutical Foundation provides financial assistance to minority undergraduate and graduate students of pharmacology, pharmaceutical science and related fields. Renewable awards ranging from $500 to $10,000 are available.

PHYSICAL THERAPY SCHOLARSHIPS

There are 185,500 physical therapists in the United States. Physical therapy is one of the fastest growing fields in the United States. Advances in orthopedic surgery have dramatically increased the demand for physical therapists. The aging of the population and the increasing use of artificial implant surgery also helps to enhance the demand for physical therapists. The demand of physical therapists is growing. Over the next decade it is expected that by 2018, there will be more than 241,000 physical therapists practicing in the United States.

Physical therapists complete a 4-year Bachelor of Science program to receive accreditation. Students who complete the bachelor's degree in another field can become qualified by earning the Masters degree in Physical Therapy.

Median annual wages of physical therapists were $72,790 in May 2008. The middle 50 percent earned between $60,300 and $85,540. The highest 10 percent earned more than $104,350.

Physical Therapist with the Bachelor of Science (BS/BSc/SB) earned $61,418 - $80,603 in their first year of practice.

American Physical Therapy Association
1111 North Fairfax Street
Alexandria, VA 22314
www.apta.org

Minority Scholarship Award
The American Physical Therapy Association provides financial assistance to outstanding undergraduate, graduate and doctoral physical therapy students. Scholarship awards of $5,000 to $15,000 are available to eligible students. The maximum total amount that can be awarded to any post professional or doctoral applicant is $52,500.

American Business Club
National Scholarship Committee
P.O. Box 5127
High Point, NC 27262
www.ambucs.com

AMBUCS offers scholarships to undergraduate students in their junior or senior year. Graduate students pursuing a master's or doctoral degree are also eligible to apply.

The AMBUCS National Scholarship Committee awards approximately $225,000 annually to students majoring in Occupational Therapy, Physical Therapy, Hearing Audiology, and Speech Language Pathology.

American Occupational Therapy Foundation Scholarships
1383 Piccard Drive, P.O. Box 1725
Rockville, MD 20850-4375
www.aotf.org

The American Occupational Therapy Foundation provides scholarships to graduate and undergraduate students on the basis of financial need and academic qualifications. Scholarship amounts vary.

The Roy and Roxie Campanella Scholarship
2880 Gateway Oaks Dr., Suite 140
Sacramento, CA 95833
Phone (916) 989-2782
www.ccapta.org/calptfund
captfund@ccapta.org

The Roy and Roxie Campanella Physical Therapist Professional Education Scholarship Program have provided financial assistance to Physical Therapy students for more than 35 years. Roy Campanella became a quadriplegic when injured in an automobile accident while he was in his prime as a catcher for the Los Angeles Dodgers. Roy and his widow Roxie became acquainted with and supportive of physical therapy following Roy's accident. The Roy and Roxie Campanella Physical Therapy Scholarship Foundation were established and have provided scholarships for qualified physical therapist students nationally.

THURGOOD MARSHAL COLLEGE FUND

Supreme Court Justice Thurgood Marshall's legacy was to ensure equal access to higher education for all. The Thurgood Marshall College Fund was established in 1987 to support exceptional scholars attending America's public historically black colleges and universities (HBCUs). The Thurgood Marshall College Fund was founded by Dr. N. Joyce Payne, Director of the Office for the Advancement of Public Black Colleges. The Thurgood Marshall College Fund is the only national organization to provide merit scholarships and program support to 47 public HBCUs. The Thurgood Marshall College Fund also supports six historically black law schools. The Thurgood Marshall College Fund has awarded more than $100 million in scholarships since 1987.

TMCF Colleges & Universities

Alabama A&M University
Alabama State University
Albany State University
Alcorn State University
Bluefield State College
Bowie State University
Central State University
Cheyney University of Pennsylvania
Chicago State University
Coppin State University
Delaware State University
Elizabeth City State University

Fayetteville State University
Florida A&M University
Florida A&M University Law School
Fort Valley State University
Grambling State University
Harris-Stowe State University
Howard University
Howard University School of Law
Jackson State University
Kentucky State University
Langston University
Lincoln University (Missouri)
Lincoln University (Pennsylvania)
Medgar Evers College
Mississippi Valley State University
Morgan State University
Norfolk State University
North Carolina A&T State University
North Carolina Central University
North Carolina Central School of Law
Prairie View A&M University
Savannah State University
South Carolina State University
Southern University and A&M College
Southern University at New Orleans
Southern University at Shreveport
Southern University Law Center
Tennessee State University
Texas Southern University

Thurgood Marshall School of Law
Tuskegee University
University of Arkansas at Pine Bluff
University of the District of Columbia
University of District of Columbia Law
University of Maryland Eastern Shore
University of the Virgin Islands
Virginia State University
West Virginia State University
Winston-Salem State University
York College

HBCU Scholarships

Bethune Cookman University
640 Mary McLeod Bethune Blvd.
Daytona Beach, FL 32114-3099
www.bethune.cookman.edu

Dr. Mary McLeod Bethune graduated from Scotia Seminary, which later became Barber Scotia College. Upon graduation, she hoped to become a missionary. Her experience as a teacher at the Haines Normal and Industrial Institute inspired her passion as an educator. The Haines Institute was founded by ex-slave Lucy Craft Laney.

Following Lucy Laney's example, Dr Bethune founded the Daytona Educational and Industrial Training School for Negro Girls in 1904 with $1.50, 6 students, and her strong Christian faith. The desks and benches were crafted from discarded boxes and scrap lumber. Despite those humble beginnings, Dr Bethune's school was soon recognized as one the best schools in Florida.

Bethune Cookman University is guided by both Christian and intellectual principles. Bethune Cookman began a formal affiliation with the United Methodist Church in 1924. The school later merged with Jacksonville's Cookman Institute to become Bethune Cookman College in 1931.

Dr. Bethune played a major role in the national desegregation movement and became the highest ranking appointee to President Franklin Roosevelt's Negro Cabinet. Dr Bethune was a founding member of the National Council of Negro Women.

Dr Bethune first priority was the continued development of Bethune Cookman College. Dr Bethune cajoled, encouraged and implored everyone that she met to support of her small school. She was successful in enlisting the support of many prominent Americans who found her endeavors worthy of their support. Early benefactors of the school included Eleanor Roosevelt, John Rockefeller and Booker T Washington. White Hall is named in honor Thomas H White, the founder of the White Sewing Machine Company.

Today Bethune Cookman University has a superior liberal arts curriculum which combines internships with religious activities and opportunities to study abroad. There are more than 3,600 undergraduate and graduate students at Bethune Cookman University.

Bethune Cookman Financial Aid Summary

Bethune Cookman University is a member institution of the United Negro College Fund. Using the most recent information available, 22% of 1st year Bethune Cookman students had their need fully met. The average award for 1st year students at Bethune Cookman was $14,175.

Bethune Cookman University Scholarships

Presidential Scholarship

The Bethune Cookman University Presidential Scholarship is awarded to incoming high school students who have demonstrated superior academic achievement. Incoming students with a minimum grade point average of 3.5 and a cumulative math and verbal SAT score of 1590-1800 eligible for this award. The Presidential Scholarship includes full tuition, fees, room and board. The Presidential Scholarship is renewable for 10 semesters.

Excelsior Scholarship

The Bethune Cookman University Excelsior Scholarship for New Freshman is awarded to students with a minimum grade point average of 3.4. A cumulative math and verbal SAT score of 1460-1680 are necessary to be eligible for this award. The Excelsior Scholarship is renewable for 8 semesters.

Academic Merit Award

The Bethune Cookman University Academic Merit Award provides tuition assistance of up to $5000 to students with a minimum grade point average of 3.0 and a cumulative math and verbal SAT score of 1350-1460. The Bethune Cookman University Academic Merit Award is renewable; however, students must reapply annually.

Spelman College
350 Spelman Lane SW
Atlanta, Georgia 30314
www.spelman.edu

Spelman College was founded in 1881 as the Atlanta Baptist Female Seminary. Instruction began at Friendship Baptist Church with 11 students, $100 and teachers from the Oread Institute, Harriet E. Giles and Sophia B. Packard.

The school was later renamed Spelman Seminary in honor of Laura Spelman, an Oread graduate and the wife of John Rockefeller. The Spelman family, devout, anti-slavery activists, was so impressed that they paid off the schools' debt and provided funds for future expansion.

Today Spelman College enrolls approximately 2,400 students and is considered one the best liberal arts colleges for women in the United States. The College has amassed an endowment fund of over $295 million, and is ranked in the top 75 of liberal arts colleges by U.S. News and World Report.

Notable Alumni like Marian Wright Edelman, Emmy Award winning actress Esther Rolle and Alice Walker, Pulitzer Prize winning author of the Color Purple, help to affirm the exemplary reputation of Spelman College.

Spelman College Financial Aid Summary

Spellman College provides comprehensive financial aid options to students with financial need and to promote high academic achievement.

Spelman College is a UNCF member college.

Using the most recent information available, 75% of full-time undergraduates at Spelman College received need based scholarships or grants. The average financial aid award for full time undergraduates at Spelman College was $24,000.

Spelman College Scholarships

Presidential Scholarship

The Spelman College Presidential Scholarship is awarded to incoming high school students who have demonstrated superior academic achievement. The Presidential Scholarship includes full tuition, fees, room and board. The Presidential Scholarship is awarded for 4 years of study.

Dean's Scholarship

The Spelman College Dean's Scholarship is awarded to approximately 65 students each year. The Dean's Scholarship varies in amounts awarded to each student. Partial and full tuition scholarships are awarded to outstanding students. The Dean's Scholarship is renewable for 4 years of study.

Dewitt Wallace Scholarship

The Dewitt Wallace Scholarship is awarded to outstanding upper class students with a record of service to the Spelman community and a minimum grade point average of 2.5. The Dewitt Wallace/Spelman College Fund was made possible with a $37 million contribution from the founder of Reader's Digest. The Dewitt Wallace Scholarship is renewable; however, students must reapply annually.

The **WISE** scholarship program is funded by the National Aeronautics and Space Administration. The program recognizes and rewards outstanding students pursuing degrees in math, science or engineering. The WISE Scholarship awards partial tuition, fees, room and board. Each summer WISE scholars participate in summer research at NASA laboratories.

Howard University
2400 Sixth Street, NW
Washington, D.C. 20059
www.howard.edu

Howard University was established by Congressional Charter in 1867. The University is named after General Oliver O. Howard, Christian Abolitionist, Civil War hero, and Commissioner of the Freedmen's Bureau.

Since its inception, Howard University has been nonsectarian and open to people of both sexes and all races. Howard's first graduates were black, white, male and female.

The University has played a unique role in American culture, the affairs of the nation and the world.

Howard University is the world's largest and most comprehensive university with a predominantly African-American enrollment. Howard University awards B.A, B.S, M.A, MBA and Ph.D. degrees, in academic fields of study. The University has its own law, divinity, social work, dentistry, and medical schools.

Howard University is one of only seventy universities to be designated a Level One Research University by the Carnegie Foundation. Howard University is the number one producer of African American Ph.D.s in the nation. More than 90% of Howard's 2,000-plus faculty holds doctoral or professional degrees.

Howard's award winning university faculty continues to produce groundbreaking research on topics not limited to, but including; cancer, sickle cell anemia, laser chemistry, and computer aided design.

There are more than 150 campus organizations, honor and professional societies, religious organizations, fraternities, and sororities.

The university operates a public television station (WHMM-TV), two university-operated radio stations (WHUR-FM and WHBC-AM), and the award winning newspaper, The Hilltop.

Howard University Financial Aid Summary

Howard University is a member of the Thurgood Marshall Scholarship Fund. Using the most recent information available, the average financial aid package for Howard University Students was $17,000. The average need based gift was $9,559 for full time undergraduates. The average award for a Howard University student with no financial need was $13,329 for 1st year students.

Howard University Scholarships

Howard University maintains a number of Institutional Scholarship Programs that seek to reward and promote high academic achievement

Trustee Scholarship
The Howard University Trustee Scholarship recognizes High academic achievement with throughout Howard University's individual schools and colleges. Awards are made annually to full time students with a minimum grade point average of 3.0. Full and half tuition grants are awarded to eligible students.

Laureate Scholarship
The Howard Laureate Scholarship provides full tuition, fees, room, board and a $950 annual book stipend to National Achievement Scholars who designate Howard University as their first college choice. The minimum grade point average for this award is 3.30 on a 4.00 grading scale.

Capstone Scholarship
The Capstone Scholarship provides full tuition, fees, and room to students who have a minimum 3.25 grade point average. The award is renewed annually.

Founders Scholarship
The Founders Scholarship provides full tuition, fees, room, board and a $500 book stipend to students with grade point average of 3.50 and above.

Legacy Scholarship
Howard University awards the Legacy Scholarship to students who achieve a minimum grade point average of 3.0. Legacy Scholars are awarded full tuition and fees.

Frederick Douglass Scholarship
The Frederick Douglass Scholars Program provides up to $75,000 in stipend support, full tuition, and research funding, for students who wish to pursue college or university teaching as a career. Frederick Douglass Scholars are required to maintain a 3.50 minimum grade point average.

Howard University Transfer Scholarship
The Howard University Transfer Scholarship is awarded to prospective transfer students who have demonstrated exceptional academic achievement. Students with 10 transferable hours and a 3.25 grade point average are eligible for full tuition scholarships. The scholarship is renewable for 3 years.

Clark Atlanta University
222 James P. Brawley Drive SW
Atlanta, Georgia, 30314
www.cau.edu

Atlanta University was founded by the American Missionary Association in 1865. Atlanta University is the Nation's oldest graduate institution with a predominately African American student body. Atlanta University has supplied the South with its teachers and librarians since the late 1870's.

Clark University was founded as Clark College in 1869 by the Methodist Episcopal Church. The school was named in honor of Bishop David Wasgett Clark. Bishop Clark was the first President of the Freedman's Aid Society of the Methodist Church. The Gannon School of Theology was established on the campus of Clark in 1883.

In 1957, the controlling Boards of the six institutions (Atlanta University; Clark, Morehouse, Morris Brown and Spelman Colleges; and Gammon Theological Seminary) ratified new Articles of Affiliation. The new contract created the Atlanta University Center.

The influence of Atlanta University has been extended through its professional journals and organizations. Dr. W.E.B. Du Bois was member of the faculty. Atlanta University Publications helped to raise the awareness and understanding of the problems affecting Black people in the Southern United States.

Today Clark Atlanta is recognized as one of the best universities in the South. Clark Atlanta was ranked on The Washington Monthly's 2008 list of "Best Colleges and Universities" Clark Atlanta University offers 40 undergraduate and 37 masters programs. There are 9 doctoral degree programs.

The University has more faculty possessing Ph.D. degrees than any other private historically Black college or university in the South

Prominent alumni include civil rights leader Ralph Abernathy, West Point graduate Henry O. Flipper, educator Marva Collins, and attorney, playwright, composer James Weldon Johnson.

Clark Atlanta University Financial Aid Summary

Clark Atlanta University is a member of the United Negro College Fund. Clark University offers extensive financial assistance to students in the form of institutional scholarships, grants, work study programs, federal and state financial assistance and guaranteed student loans. Clark Atlanta University uses an online application and verification process to determine financial awards to students.

Using the most recent information available, 42% of full time undergraduate students with financial need had their need fully met. The average financial aid package for full time undergraduate students at Clark Atlanta was $10,935.The average gift award for Clark Atlanta students with financial need was $3,818.

Clark Atlanta University Scholarships

Provost Academic Achievers Award

The Clark Atlanta Provost Academic Achievers Award seeks to recognize and reward high academic achievement. Students with a minimum grade point average of 3.5 and a cumulative math and verbal SAT score of 1200 are eligible for the Provost Academic Achiever Award. The Provost Academic Achievers Award includes full tuition, fees, room and board. The Award is renewable for 4 years.

Presidential Scholarship

The Clark Atlanta University Presidential Scholarship is awarded to incoming high school students who have demonstrated superior academic achievement. Students with a minimum grade point average of 3.75 and a cumulative math and verbal SAT score of 1300 eligible for this award. The Presidential Scholarship includes full tuition, fees, room and board. The Presidential Scholarship is renewable for 4 years of study.

Lincoln University
1570 Baltimore Pike,
Lincoln University, PA 19352
www.lincoln.edu

History

Lincoln University was founded as the Ashmun Institute in 1854 by Rev. John Miller Dickey, a Presbyterian minister, and his wife, Sarah Emlen Cresson. The school was supported by the American Colonization Society. The Ashmun Institute was renamed Lincoln University in 1866 after the assassination of President Abraham Lincoln.

Many Christians in the Abolition Movement felt that America's Blacks once free would continue to be stigmatized by their race. Abolitionist, Henry Clay described the Freed Slaves dilemma as an "unconquerable prejudice resulting from their color, they never could amalgamate with the free whites of this country.

The first graduating class of Lincoln University, James R. Amos, his brother Thomas H. Amos, and Armistead Miller sailed for Liberia in April 1859.

President Isaac Norton Rendall, a graduate of Princeton University and its Seminary, modeled the

Lincoln Curricula on his experiences from Princeton University.

Under the leadership of President Isaac Norton Rendall, Lincoln became a center of academic excellence. At one point, Lincoln graduated approximately 20 percent of the Black physicians and more than 10 percent of the Black attorneys in the United States during the first one hundred years of its existence. In fact, Lincoln University operated Schools of Law and Medicine until 1873.

Lincoln University offers its approximately 2,000 students, 37 undergraduate majors, 22 undergraduate minors, and 5 Pre-Professional (Dentistry, Engineering, Law, Medicine, and Veterinary Science) programs.

Today, Lincoln University provides a liberal arts and science-based undergraduate core curriculum and select graduate programs to prepare students of all races and nationality.

Notable Alumni include Thurgood Marshall, Langston Hughes, and Kwame Nkrumah the first Prime Minister of Ghana. Lincoln University Alumni have served as United States Ambassadors or Mission Chiefs in more than 10 countries.

Lincoln University Financial Aid Summary

Lincoln University is a member of the Thurgood Marshall Fund. Lincoln University offers extensive financial assistance to students in the form of institutional scholarships, grants, work study programs, federal and state financial assistance and guaranteed student loans.

Using the most recent information available the average financial aid package for Lincoln University Students was $9,118. The average award for a Lincoln student with no financial need was $8,509.

Lincoln University Scholarships

Lincoln University maintains a comprehensive scholarship and financial aid program for incoming and current students. The Lincoln University rewards and recognizes outstanding academic achievement with several scholarship programs.

Lincoln University Merit Awards

The Lincoln University Merit Award provides $5,500 tuition grants to students with a minimum grade point average of 3.5. Lincoln University students with a grade point average of 3.3-3.4 are eligible for tuition grants of $4,000. Lincoln Students with a minimum grade point average of 3.0-3.29. are awarded $2,500 tuition grants. The Lincoln University merit award is renewable for 3 years.

Morgan State University
1700 East Cold Spring lane
Baltimore, MD 21251
www.morgan.edu

Morgan State University was founded in 1867 as the Centenary Biblical Institute. The school was established by the Methodist Episcopal Church for the training of young men for career in the ministry. The school was renamed Morgan College in 1890 in honor of Rev Lyttleton Morgan, Chairman of the Board of Trustees.

Substantial contributions by Andrew Carnegie in 1915 allowed the school to move to its current location settle all debts and complete construction of the central academic building.

Today, Morgan State University is part of the University of Maryland system. More than 6,500 students are enrolled at MSU.

Morgan State is one of the leading schools in the nation in graduating students who goes on to earn a Doctoral degree. The University offers the Masters of Business Administration in Accounting, Finance, Information Systems, Management, Marketing, and Taxation.

Morgan State University also awards Master of Science degrees in Biology, Chemistry, and Physics. The Morgan State University School of Engineering began instruction in 1984. The Doctor of Engineering Degree is offered in Civil, electrical, and Industrial Engineering.

Morgan State University Scholarships

University Honors Program

The Morgan State University Honors Program provides significant financial support to students who meet and maintain specific academic standards. Honors Program Scholarships average $13,500.

Gateway Scholarship

The Gateway Scholarship is awarded to students with a minimum grade point average of 3.0. A cumulative math and verbal SAT score of 1000 is necessary to be eligible for this award. The Gateway Scholarship is renewable for 8 semesters.

Deans Scholarship

The Morgan State University Deans Scholarship is awarded to high school students who have demonstrated superior academic achievement. Students with a minimum grade point average of 3.4 and a cumulative math and verbal SAT score of 1200 are eligible for this award. The Morgan State

University Deans Scholarship awards $7,500 per semester towards tuition, fees, room and board.

Regents Scholarship

The Morgan State University Regents Scholarship is awarded to incoming high school students who have demonstrated superior academic achievement. Incoming students with a minimum grade point average of 3.6 and a cumulative math and verbal SAT score of 1300 eligible for this award. The Regents Scholarship includes full tuition, fees, room and board. The Regents Scholarship is renewable for 8 semesters of study with satisfactory academic progress.

Grambling State University
403 Main Street
Grambling, LA 71245
www.gram.edu

History

Grambling State University emerged from the desire of black farmers in rural northern Louisiana who wanted to help educate others in North and West Louisiana. In 1896 the North Louisiana Colored Agriculture Relief Association was formed to organize and operate a school

The North Louisiana Colored Agriculture Relief Association purchased a two-story building and 23-acres of land from a local African American farmer. The school began instruction in 1901 as the Colored Industrial and Agricultural School.

Tuskegee Institute graduate Charles Adams, with the assistance and direction of Booker T Washington was Grambling's' founder and 1st school President.

In 1905, the School moved to its present location on a 200-acre plot, parcel. The school was reorganized using Tuskegee as a model, and renamed the North Louisiana Agricultural and Industrial School.

The school was renamed Grambling College in 1946, after sawmill owner P. G. Grambling donated land to aid in the schools construction and expansion.

Today the campus of Grambling State University sits on more than 380 acres. Grambling State University is a constituent member of the University of Louisiana system.

The University awards the associates, and bachelor's degrees in the Schools of Arts and Sciences, Business, and Education.

The Grambling State University School of Graduate Studies and Research offers master and doctoral degrees. Grambling offers the only doctorate in developmental education in the nation

Grambling State Financial Aid Summary

Grambling State University is a member of the Thurgood Marshal Scholarship Fund.
The average financial aid package for full time undergraduates at Grambling State University is $$6800. The average need based gift was $2928 for full time undergraduates. The average award for a Grambling State University student with no financial need was $2328.

Grambling State University Scholarships

Presidential Scholarship

The Grambling University Presidential Scholarship is awarded to high school students who have demonstrated superior academic achievement. Students with a minimum GPA of 3.5 and a cumulative math and verbal SAT score of 1210-1230 are eligible for this award. The Presidential Scholarship includes full tuition, fees, room and board.

Executive Merit Scholarship

The Grambling State University Executive Merit Scholarship is awarded to students selected Valedictorian or Salutatorian of select High Schools that have participated in Grambling's Upward Bound Program. The Executive Merit Scholarship includes full tuition, fees, room and board.

Academic Achievement Award

The Grambling State University awards the Academic Achievement Award to students that have a minimum GPA of 3.0 and a cumulative math and verbal SAT score of 940 and above.

The Academic Achievement Award provides tuition grants of up to $3,000 per year. Academic Achievement Awards are renewable on an annually if the student maintains a full academic course load and a minimum grade point average of 3.0.

Texas Southern University
300 Clegburne Avenue
Houston Texas 77004
www.tsu.edu

The Houston College for Negroes was purchased by the state of Texas, and renamed the Texas State University for Negroes on March 3, 1947. In February of the 1946, Herman Marion Sweatt applied to the University Of Texas School Of Law. The University Of Texas School Of Law denied his admission due to his race. Herman Sweatt filed suit against the University of Texas, as he was more than qualified as a candidate for admission.

The state created the Texas State University in order to provide separate but equal educational institution that would allow the state to legally allow the University of Texas to remain a Whites' only School.

The Texas State University for Negroes awarded its first Doctor of Jurisprudence Degree in 1950. The University has awarded more than 40,000 degrees in its 57 year history.

Today, Texas Southern University is one of the most ethnically diverse schools in the nation. The campus now covers more than 150 acres, with approximately 9500 students.

The Texas Southern university is comprised of ten schools and colleges, including the Graduate School, College of Liberal Arts and Behavioral Sciences, the Barbara Jordan-Mickey Leland School of Public Affairs, the College of Pharmacy and Health Sciences, the College of Education, the Jesse H. Jones School of Business, the College of Continuing Education, the Tavis Smiley School of Communication, the College of Science and Technology, and the Thurgood Marshall School of Law. Texas Southern awards the Bachelors, Masters, Doctoral and the Doctor of Jurisprudence.

Texas Southern Financial Aid Summary

Using the most recent information available, 28% of 1st year Texas Southern students had their financial need fully met. The average financial aid package for 1st year students at Texas Southern was $14,065.

Texas Southern Scholarships

Texas Southern University provides a number of scholarships for deserving students. The University awards scholarships to students who major in Business, Science, Computer Science, Mathematics and Biology. Eligibility requirements vary by field of study. University Scholarships of up to $10,000 are available.

Morehouse University
830 Westview Drive, Southwest
Atlanta, Georgia 30314

Morehouse University is a private, male HBCU in Atlanta, Georgia. The school enrolls approximately 3,000 male students. The 61 acre campus is part of the Atlanta University system. All tenured faculty at the University hold terminal degrees.

Morehouse College was founded in 1867 as the Augusta Institute by William Jefferson White, with the support of former slave Reverend Richard C. Coulter. The first classes of the Augusta Institute were held at the Springfield Baptist Church. In 1885, with a gift from John D. Rockefeller, the school moved to its current location.

Dr Benjamin Elijah Mayes, a Phi Beta Kappa graduate of Bates College and the University of Chicago became the President of Morehouse College in 1940. A mentor of Martin Luther King Jr., Dr Mayes' inspiration would elevate the Colleges reputation and international enrollment. Dr Mayes served as the founding advisor to the Psi Chapter of the Omega Psi Phi Fraternity.

Today Morehouse University is regularly recognized by the Wall Street Journal and Black Enterprise Magazine as one of the Best Colleges in America.

Morehouse students have been awarded Rhodes and Fulbright Scholarships. The Wall Street Journal recognizes Morehouse University as one of the top "feeder schools" nationwide for elite graduate study.

Morehouse University is part of the Atlanta University Center, which includes Spellman College, Clark Atlanta University and the Morehouse Medical School. Prominent Alumni include Noble Peace Prize Winner Martin Luther King Jr., NAACP President Julian Bond, US Surgeon General David Satcher, Spike Lee, Congressman Earl Hilliard, Sanford Bishop and actor Samuel Jackson.

Morehouse University Financial Aid Summary

Using the most recent information available, 100% of Morehouse Students with financial need received some form of assistance. The majority of financial assistance awarded to Morehouse students was in the form of scholarships and grants (58%). Approximately 200 Morehouse University students had their need fully met. The average award for a Morehouse student with financial need was $13,984. The average award for a Morehouse student with no financial need was $9,559. Morehouse University is a member of the UNCF. Morehouse University students are eligible to receive, upon application, financial assistance from the United Negro College Fund.

Fisk University
1000 17th Avenue, North
Nashville, Tennessee
www.fisk.edu

History

Fisk was established by John Ogden, Reverend Erastus Milo Cravath, and Reverend Edward P. Smith. Fisk University was named in honor of General Clinton B. Fisk of the Tennessee Freedmen's Bureau. Instruction began on January 9, 1866. The school is affiliated with United Church of Christ

As devout Christian abolitionists, the men were committed helping to educate the newly freed slaves. The first students, who ranged in age from seven to seventy, began their education in former Union army barracks near the present site of Nashville's Union Station. Instruction began on January 9, 1866. In 1871, Fisk began offering instruction at the college level, and in 1875, it offered its first bachelor's degree.

The University is known for its famous Jubilee Singers, who began to perform nationally and internationally in 1876 to bring needed money to the school. The Jubilee Singers have performed at the White House, the World Peace Conference, and before Queen Victoria and Kaiser Wilhelm of Europe. In 1976, Jubilee Hall, the first permanent building of higher education for southern blacks, was designated a national landmark. The Fisk campus was named as a national historic district in 1978 by the U.S. Department of Interior in recognition of its unique place in history, art, and culture.

Today, Fisk University is a 4 year, private, historically Black University that awards the Bachelor's and Master's degree. Fisk has a world renowned reputation of excellence. Fisk attracts students from around the world. Fisk University contributes more alumni to the ranks of African-American scholars prepared for Doctoral study than any other institution, Black or White, in the U.S. Among currently practicing Black physicians, lawyers, and dentists, one in six is a Fisk graduate.

W.E.B. DuBois, the first Harvard PhD, author, and co-founder of the NAACP is a noted Fisk alumnus.

Fisk University Financial Aid Summary

Fisk University is a member of the UNCF.
Using the most recent information available the average financial aid package for Fisk University students was $13,650. The average gift award for a Fisk student with financial need was $3,700. The average gift award for a Fisk student with no financial need was $8,200.

Fisk University Scholarships

Presidential Scholarship

The Fisk University Presidential Scholarship is awarded to students who graduate in the top 5% of their classes. Students must possess a grade point average of 4.0., and a cumulative math and verbal SAT score of 1260. The Presidential Scholarship includes full tuition, fees, room and board. The scholarship is renewable for three years. Fisk Presidential Scholars must maintain a cumulative GPA of 3.3 in order to have the scholarship renewed.

Dean's Academic Scholarship

The Dean's Academic Scholarship is awarded to students who graduate in the top 10% of their classes. Students must possess a grade point average range of 3.5-3-9 and a cumulative math and verbal SAT score of 1150. The recipient of the Dean's Academic Scholarship will be awarded full tuition and fees. The scholarship is renewable for three years. Students must maintain a cumulative GPA of 3.3 in order to have the scholarship renewed.

General Academic Scholarship

The Fisk University General Academic Scholarship is awarded to students with strong leadership potential and community involvement. Eligible, students must possess a grade point average range of 3.3-349 and competitive SAT scores. The scholarship is renewable for three years. Recipients must maintain a cumulative GPA of 3.3 for renewal of the scholarship. Tuition awards of $3000 are provided to Fisk University General Academic Scholar

Hampton University
Hampton, Virginia 23668
www.hampton.edu

History

Located in the tidewater area of Virginia between Virginia Beach and Williamsburg, Hampton University was originally founded as the Hampton Normal and Industrial Institute in 1868 as a place to train newly freed slaves. A private, nonsectarian, coeducational institution of higher learning, Hampton was the first US College to admit Native Americans.

Today, Hampton is regularly rated as one of the Best colleges for African Americans by Black Enterprise Magazine. Hampton University has grown into a comprehensive university offering a broad range of technical, liberal arts, pre-professional, professional and graduate degree programs.
Hampton has over 5,700 students. Most live on one of the nation's most beautiful campuses. The University has erected 14 new buildings and spent more than $35,000,000 on the renovation of its historic facilities. The Hampton Harbor Project is a university-owned commercial development. The shopping center and 246 apartments' profits are utilized to finance student scholarships.

During the Civil War, Union-held Fort Monroe in Hampton Roads became a gathering point and safe haven for fugitive slaves. The fugitive slaves were considered "contraband of War by the commander, General Benjamin F. Butler, and thereby safe from return to slave owners. General Butler's "Contraband Army" built the Grand Contraband Camp nearby from materials reclaimed from the ruins of Hampton, which was burned down by retreating Confederate Rebels.

Mary Smith Peake taught the first classes on September 17, 1861, under the Emancipation Oak tree in defiance of a Virginia law against teaching slaves, free blacks and mulattos to read or write. U.S. President Abraham Lincoln's Emancipation Proclamation was read to local freedmen under the Emancipation Oak, which is still located on the campus today.

After the Civil War, a normal school was established in 1868, a Quaker, and devout abolitionist and former Union Brigadier General Samuel C. Armstrong as its first principal. The school was established on the grounds of the Little Scotland plantation.

Hampton received much of its financial support in the years following the Civil War from church groups and former officers and soldiers of the Union Army. General William Jackson Palmer, a Union cavalry commander from Philadelphia, and Medal of Honor Recipient, gave substantial sums to the school. A Quaker and a pacifist, William Palmer's abhorrence for slavery compelled him to enter the War.

As President, General Sam Armstrong, the son of a missionary, felt it was important to add the skills necessary to be self-supporting in the impoverished South. Under his guidance, a Hampton education became well-known as an education that combined cultural uplift with moral and manual training. Hampton Institute would provide an education that encompassed "the head, the heart, and the hands."

Hampton University Financial Aid Summary

Hampton University is a member of the Thurgood Marshal Scholarship Fund. Using the most recent information available, 37% of full time undergraduate students had their need fully met. The average financial aid package for full time undergraduates at Hampton University is $4704. The average need based gift was $3844 for full time undergraduates. The average award for a Hampton University student with no financial need was $11,422.

Hampton University Scholarships

Hampton University provides a number of scholarships to incoming students. The University rewards and recognizes outstanding academic achievement with several scholarship programs.

Trustee Scholarship

The Trustee Scholarship is a 4 year scholarship that includes tuition room board and a book stipend, and computer to outstanding students that score a minimum of 1400 on the SAT.

Presidential Scholarships

The Hampton University Presidential Scholarships provides full tuition room and board to students that score 1300-1390 on the SAT.

Hampton Scholars

The Hampton Scholars program awards a 4 year full tuition scholarship to students that score 1200-1290 on the SAT.

Merit Achievement Scholarship

The Hampton University Merit Achievement Scholarship offers a partial tuition scholarship to students who score 1100-1190 on the SAT.

Florida A&M University
Wahnish Way & Gamble Street
Tallahassee, FL 32307
www.famu.edu

Florida Agricultural & Mechanical University was founded in 1887 as the State Normal College for Colored Students. The school began instruction with fifteen students and two instructors.

Today, Florida Agricultural & Mechanical University is a four-year, public, co-educational and fully accredited institution. Approximately 10,000 students are enrolled.

The main campus extends over 419 acres. There are 12 schools and colleges. Florida Agricultural & Mechanical University operated a College of Law from 1954 to 1968. The University is rich in history. After a suspicious fire on campus, Andrew Carnegie donated $10,000 to help the school rebuild. Carnegie Library is the only such library on the campus of an African American land-grant college.
Florida Agricultural & Mechanical University offers more 60 bachelors' degrees in over 100 major fields of study. The Graduate school awards 36 Master's degrees.

There are eleven Doctoral programs currently at Florida A&M University.

Time Magazine recognized Florida A&M as "College of the Year" in 1997. Today, FAMU awards more baccalaureate degrees to African-Americans than any other institution in the nation.

Florida A&M has been recognized on more than one occasion as the number-one college for African Americans in the country by Black Enterprise Magazine.

Each year FAMU recruits and enrolls more African American National Achievement Scholars than any other public university in the United States.

Florida A&M University Financial Aid Summary

Florida A&M University is a member of the Thurgood Marshal Scholarship Fund. Using the most recent information available, 25% of full time undergraduate students had their financial need fully met. The average financial aid package for full time undergraduates at Florida A&M University is $10,478. The average need based gift was $7498 for full time undergraduates. The average award for a Florida A&M University student with no financial need was $8929.

Florida A&M University Scholarships

Distinguished Scholars Award

The Distinguished Scholars Award is a 4 year undergraduate scholarship. Incoming freshman students with a minimum grade point average of 3.5 and a cumulative math and verbal SAT score of 1200 are eligible. The Distinguished Scholars Award includes full tuition, fees, room and board.

Presidents Special Scholarship

The Florida A&M University Presidents Special Scholarship is a 4 year undergraduate scholarship. Tuition scholarships of $6000 are awarded to students with a minimum grade point average of 3.0 and a cumulative math and verbal SAT score of 1190.

Florida A&M University maintains a comprehensive financial aid program. Scholarships are awarded to students majoring in Education, Biology, Chemistry, Mathematics, Computer Science, Engineering, Business, Pre-Medical Studies and Journalism.

The Florida A&M University Adopted High School Award is offered to students selected Valedictorian or Salutatorian of his or her graduating class. The Florida A&M University Adopted High School Award includes full tuition, fees, room and board.

Southern University and A&M College
Baton Rouge, Louisiana 70813
www.subr.edu

Southern University was chartered in April 1880. P.B.S Pinchback, T.T. Allain, and Henry Demas, African American delegates to the Louisiana State Constitutional Convention proposed that an institution "for the education of persons of color" be established during the 1879 session. The school began instruction with 12 students in New Orleans in March, 1881. Southern University became a Land Grant College in 1890. Needing room to expand, the school moved north of Baton Rouge to Scotlandville, Louisiana, in 1914. Southern University is part of the nation's only historically Black Land Grant university system in the U.S. Southern University has campuses in New Orleans and Shreveport.

Dr. Joseph Samuel Clark became the first president on Southern University in Baton Rouge. Dr Clark presided over much of the early construction of the campus. Upon his retirement in 1938, Southern University enrolled approximately 500 students. Dr Felton Clark began his tenure as president shortly after the retirement of his father, Dr Joseph Clark. Dr Felton Clark saw the campus expand to more than 500 acres and 10,000 students during his 30 year career. The Louisiana State University refused to admit African American to its Law School. The Southern University Law was created in 1947. Southern University Law School is one of the most diverse schools in the United States.

The Southern University System was established in 1974. Approximately 10,000 students attend Southern University today. Southern University graduates more African-American students in engineering, technology, computer science, and math than from any other university system in the nation.

The Southern University Graduate program confers Master's and Doctoral degrees. There are Doctoral programs in the following fields of study biomedical science, material science, math and science education, nursing, public policy, and urban forestry.

Southern University Financial Aid Summary
Using the most recent information available, 21% full time undergraduates at Southern University had their need fully met. The average financial package for students at Southern University was $9,516 for full time undergraduates.

North Carolina Central University
1801 Fayetteville Street
Durham, North Carolina 27707
www.nccu.edu

The North Carolina College for Negroes (NCCU) was chartered in 1909 and opened in 1910 as the National Religious Training School and Chautauqua under the leadership of President James E. Shepard.

In 1923, the school was acquired by the state of North Carolina and renamed Durham State Normal School.

The schools mission and name changed in 1925, the North Carolina College for Negroes (NCC), became the first state-supported African-American liberal arts college in the United States.

The Graduate School began instruction in 1940. The North Carolina College for Negroes Law School opened its doors in 1940 as well. In 1947, the college was renamed North Carolina College at Durham.

Today, North Carolina Central University is part of the 16 member University of North Carolina System.

The NCCU School of Law completed a major renovation in 2005. The building is now one of the largest public law school facilities in the Southeast United States.

North Carolina Central Financial Aid Summary

Using the most recent information available, 35% of first year North Carolina Central University students with financial need had their need fully met. The average award for full time students at North Carolina Central University was $7,144.

North Carolina Central University Scholarships

Soaring Eagle Scholarship

The North Carolina Central University Soaring Eagle Scholarship is awarded to National Merit semifinalist with a minimum grade point average of 3.5 and a cumulative math and verbal SAT score of 1900. The North Carolina Central University Soaring Eagle Scholarship includes full tuition, fees, room and board. A $500 per semester stipend is included.

Rising Eagle Scholarship

The North Carolina Central University Rising Eagle Scholarship is awarded to incoming high school students with a minimum grade point average of 3.5 and a cumulative math and verbal SAT score of 1800. The North Carolina Central University Rising Eagle Scholarship is a 4 year award. The North Carolina Central University Rising Eagle Scholarship provides a $500 per semester stipend, full tuition, fees, and room and board.

Tuskegee University
Tuskegee, AL 36088
www.tuskegee.edu

Tuskegee University was founded in 1881 as the Normal School for Colored Teachers. Tuskegee was result of the inspired actions of a former slave Lewis Adams and George W Campbell, a former slave owner. The men were concerned that the newly freed men would be unable to support themselves without a means of acquiring an education.

The men were able to obtain financial assistance from Alabama State Senator W. F. Foster after his election to office. Lewis Adams and George Campbell helped to organize voters in support of Foster's Senate campaign. Once in office Senator Foster worked with fellow legislator Arthur L. Brooks to draft and pass legislation authorizing $2,000 to create the school.

The first class was taught by Dr Booker T Washington on July 4th, 1881 in a building provided by Butler AME Zion Church. Dr Booker T Washington, a former slave, was a graduate of Wayland Seminary and Hampton Institute.

Dr Washington purchased 100 acres in Macon, Alabama and moved the school to the site of a former plantation the following year. Dr Washington felt that self reliance was vital to the survival of the freedman. The majority of the buildings on campus were constructed by Tuskegee Students.

Tuskegee now has more than 3,200 students on a campus that includes some 5,500 acres (the main campus, farm, and forest land) and more than 70 buildings.

The Tuskegee University has a fully accredited College of Veterinary Medicine that awards the Doctoral Degree. Tuskegee has one of the oldest nursing programs in the United States.

The school produces the largest number of African Americans graduates with baccalaureate degrees in math, science, and engineering in Alabama.

Tuskegee University has produced more African-American military officers than any other institution. The famed Tuskegee Airmen are part of this legacy of excellence and patriotism.

Tuskegee University Financial Aid Summary
Using the most recent information available, approximately 70% of 1st year Tuskegee students had their financial need fully met. The average award for 1st year students at Tuskegee was $13,824 for full time undergraduates. The average gift award for a Tuskegee student with financial need was $8,000. The average gift award for a Tuskegee student with no financial need was $6,000.

Lincoln University
820 Chestnut Street, Jefferson City, MO 65101
www.lincolnu.edu

Lincoln University was founded in 1866 by Union Soldiers and Officers of the 62nd United States Colored Infantry. The 62nd United States Colored Infantry was stationed at Fort McIntosh, Texas; however the 62nd was comprised predominately by soldiers, who were ex slaves and free men of color from Missouri.

The school was established in Jefferson City, Missouri. The school was designated for the special benefit of freed slaves. The school was financed with a contribution of $5,000 by the members of the 62nd Colored Infantry. An additional contribution of $1,400 was provided by the soldiers of the 65th United States Colored Infantry. The school began instruction in an old frame building as Lincoln Institute on September 17th, 1866. Richard Baxter Foster was named first principal of Lincoln Institute. Richard Foster was formerly a 1st Lieutenant in the 62nd United States Colored Infantry.

The school moved to its current campus location in 1869. The state of Missouri began to support teacher training at Lincoln Institute in 1870. Lincoln Institute became a land grant institution in 1890.

Walthall M. Moore, the first African American representative in the Missouri State legislature, introduced the bill that would grant University status to Lincoln Institute in 1921.

Graduate instruction began in 1940. The School of Journalism was established in 1942. In 1954, after the United States Supreme Court ruled on the Brown v. Board of Education case, Lincoln University responded. Today, Lincoln University is one of the most diverse schools in the United States.

Lincoln University Financial Aid Summary

Using the most recent information available, more than 15% of full time undergraduate at Lincoln University had their need fully met. The average financial aid package for award for full time undergraduates at Lincoln University was $8,000. The average gift award for a Lincoln University student with financial need was $3,000.

Lincoln University Scholarships

Lincoln University maintains a comprehensive financial aid program that seeks to address the needs of all students.

Curator Scholarship

Lincoln University awards the Curator Scholarship to graduates of accredited high schools in the state of

Missouri. Students who graduate in the top 10% of their class with a minimum ACT score of 24 are eligible for the Curator Scholarship. The Curator Scholarship provides an award the includes 90% of tuition, a $900 book voucher, The Curator Scholarship is renewable for students who maintain a grade point average of 3.2 and a full time academic course load.

Presidential Scholarship
The Lincoln University Presidential Scholarship is awarded to incoming high school students who graduate in the top 15% of their class with a minimum ACT score of 21. The Presidential Scholarship provides an award equal to 80% of tuition, $2000 towards room and board, and an $800 book voucher. The Presidential Scholarship is renewable for students who maintain a grade point average of 3.1 and a full time academic course load.

Lincoln University Institutional Scholarships
Lincoln University Institutional Scholarships are awarded to students who have completed 30 or credits of college or university coursework. Transfer students and current students are eligible to apply. The Lincoln University Institutional Scholarships provides an award that includes 70% of tuition, $1500 towards room and board, and an $800 book and supplies voucher.

Dillard University
2601 Gentilly Blvd
New Orleans, LA 70122

Dillard University was formed in 1934 after the merger of Straight College and New Orleans University. Straight College was established in 1868 by the American Missionary Association. The school was named in honor of Seymour Straight who provided an endowment for the University. Straight University was open to all races. The University operated a Law Department until 1886. Straight University operated a medical school as well. Dr James W. Ames, a Straight Medical Alumnus, established the first hospital for blacks in Detroit in 1910. Dr Ames and Dunbar Hospital were vitally important to Detroit citizens of color. Hospitals in Detroit would not admit blacks, nor would they allow Black physicians to see black patients at their facilities.

The Straight Law Department produced Attorneys who practiced before the Supreme Court. Louis Andre' Martinet was an Attorney and Straight Law Graduate. Louis Andre' Martinet was a founder of the Comite'des Citoyens. The Comite' des Citoyens were instrumental in bringing the Plessy v. Ferguson case before the Supreme Court. P.B. S Pinchback was a Straight Graduate and the first Black Governor to serve in the continental United States.

New Orleans University was founded as Union Normal school in 1868 by the Freedman's Aid Society of the Methodist Episcopal Church. New Orleans University operated the School of Pharmacy, Flint Medical College and the Sarah Goodridge Hospital and Nurse Training School.

Today, approximately 800 students attend Dillard University. The school is located in a suburban setting in the Gentilly District of New Orleans.

Dillard University offers Bachelor of Arts and Bachelor of Science degrees in over 35 majors.

Dillard University Financial Aid Summary

Approximately 81% of full time undergraduate students had their need fully met. The average financial aid package for full time undergraduates at Dillard University is $15,241.

Dillard University Scholarships

Dillard University offers a number of scholarships awards to encourage and reward academic excellence. Dillard University awards merit scholarships to incoming freshman and transfer students based upon the student's academic promise and personal achievement.

Dillard University Scholarship

The Dillard University Scholarship is awarded to incoming high school students of superior academic achievement. The Dillard University Scholar Award provides full tuition, fees, room and board for four years. The Dillard University Scholar Award is renewable for six semesters of study. Students must maintain their GPA to be eligible for renewal.

Dillard University Presidential Scholarship

The Dillard University Presidential Scholarship is awarded to incoming high school students of outstanding academic achievement. The Presidential Scholar Award provides full tuition and fees for four years. The Dillard University Presidential Scholar Award is renewable for six semesters of study. Students must maintain an acceptable GPA to be eligible for renewal.

Dillard University Dean's Scholarship

The Dillard University Dean's Scholarship is awarded to incoming high school students of demonstrated superior academic achievement. The Dillard University Dean's Scholar Award is half-tuition. The Dillard University Dean's Scholar Award is renewable for six semesters of study.

Dillard University Merit Scholarship

The Dillard University Merit Scholarship is awarded to incoming high school students who have demonstrated superior academic achievement. The Dillard University Merit Scholar Award is $4,500. The Dillard University Merit Scholar Award is renewable for six semesters of study. Students must maintain an acceptable GPA for renewal.

Transfer Student Awards

The Dillard University Transfer Scholarship is awarded to incoming transfer students who have demonstrated superior academic achievement. The Dillard Transfer University Scholar Award provides full tuition, fees, room and board. The **Dillard Transfer University Scholar Award** is renewable for up to four semesters of study. Eligible transfer students must have a minimum of 24 or more transferable credit hours earned within the last two years. Students must maintain an acceptable GPA to be eligible for renewal.

The Dillard University Presidential Scholarship is awarded to incoming transfer students who have demonstrated superior academic achievement. The Transfer Presidential Scholar Award provides full tuition and fees. The **Dillard University Transfer Presidential Scholar Award** is renewable for up to four semesters of study. Eligible transfer students must have a minimum of 24 or more transferable credit hours earned within the last two years. Students must maintain an acceptable GPA to be eligible for renewal

The Transfer Dean's Scholarship is awarded to transfer students who have demonstrated superior academic achievement. The **Dillard University Transfer Dean's Scholar Award** is half-tuition. The Dillard University Transfer Dean's Scholar Award is renewable for up to four semesters of study. Eligible transfer students must have a minimum of 24 or more transferable credit hours earned within the last two years. Students must maintain an acceptable GPA to be eligible for renewal.

State Higher Education Agencies

Many states provide financial assistance in the form of scholarships, grants and fellowships to state residents and students that attend state supported schools. There are a number of states that provide assistance for undergraduate, graduate and professional school including law and medical school.

Alabama Commission on Higher Education
1-800-960-7773
www.ache.state.al.us

Arkansas Department of Higher Education
1-800-54-STUDY
www.arkansashighered.com

California Student Aid Commission
1-888-224-7268
www.csac.ca.gov

District of Columbia
State Education Office (District of Columbia)
202-727-6436
www.seo.dc.gov

Delaware Higher Education Commission
1-800-292-7935
www.doe.state.de.us/high-ed

Florida Department of Education
Office of Student Financial Assistance
1-888-827-2004
www.floridastudentfinancialaid.org

Georgia Student Finance Commission
1-800-505-4732
www.gsfc.org

Illinois Student Assistance Commission
1-800-899-4722
www.collegezone.com

State Student Assistance
Commission of Indiana
1-888-528-4719
www.in.gov/ssaci

Kansas Board of Regents
785-296-3421
www.kansasregents.org

Kentucky Higher Education Assistance
1-800-928-8926
www.kheaa.com

Louisiana
Office of Student Financial Assistance
1-800-259-5626
www.osfa.state.la.us

Maryland Higher Education Commission
1-800-974-1024
www.mhec.state.md.us

Mississippi Office of Student Financial Aid
1-800-327-2980
www.ihl.state.ms.us/financialaid

Missouri Department of Higher Education
1-800-473-6757
www.dhe.mo.gov

New Jersey
Higher Education Student Authority
1-800-792-8670
www.hesaa.org

New York State Higher Education Corporation
1-888-697-4372
www.hesc.org

College Foundation of North Carolina
1-866-866-2362
www.cfnc.org

Ohio Board of Regents
1-888-833-1133
1-877-428-8246 www.regents.state.oh.us/sgs

Pennsylvania Higher Education Agency
1-800-692-7392
www.pheaa.org

South Carolina Commission on Higher Ed.
803-737-2260
www.che.sc.gov

Tennessee Student Assistance Corporation
1-800-342-1663
www.collegepaystn.com

Texas Higher Education Coordinating Board
Texas Financial Aid Information Center
1-888-311-8881
www.collegefortexans.com

State Council of Higher Education for Virginia
1-877-516-0138
www.schev.edu

West Virginia Higher Education Policy Commission
1-888-825-5707
www.hepc.wvnet.edu

Puerto Rico Council on Higher Education
787-724-7100
www.ces.gobierno.pr

Virgin Islands Board of Education
340-774-0100
www.doe.vi